"I savored this book. The story is captivating, the characters feel like real people, and the insightful mirror it holds up for self-discovery and coaching are remarkable. I highly recommend it!"

—**Barry Rellaford,** co-founder, FranklinCovey Trust Practice and co-author of *A Slice of Trust*

. . . . . . . . . . .

"Donna Zajonc's beautifully written book is a roadmap to living with an empowered mindset. I truly hope it finds its way into the hands of coaches, therapists, and physicians, as well as anyone interested in changing their mind for good."

—**Carolyn Piver Dukarm**, MD, author of *Pieces of a Puzzle: The Link between Eating Disorders and ADD*

. . . . . . . . . . .

"Over the years, bringing TED* (*The Empowerment Dynamic) to practitioners and trainers, I have seen no one do this work more earnestly than Donna Zajonc. The depth of her experience springs to life in this marvelous story whose characters are strong Creators doing their inner work in order to be of service in the outer world."

—**David Emerald,** Author of *The Power of TED* (*The Empowerment Dynamic)* and *3 Vital Questions: Transforming Workplace Drama*

. . . . . . . . . . .

"Every now and then a book comes along that explains exactly how to elevate who we are as leaders and as individuals. For the last ten years, The Empowerment Dynamic has been our team's most referenced tool. Donna Zajonc's *Who Do You Want to Be* is a master class in TED* that will strengthen our journey to elevate the lives of others with love and impact. Donna, thank you for providing such an incredible guide to reach our destination."

—**Lori Fightmaster,** Chief Learning and Diversity Officer, First United Bank

"I will be sharing Donna's book with every leader I work with, from manager to CEO. It's a must-read for developing the mindset of leadership."

—**Jenn Lofgren**, MCC, Incito Executive and Leadership Development, *Forbes* Contributor

. . . . . . . . . . .

"The Empowerment Dynamic has become the foundation of our conscious leadership program, empowering us to collaborate creatively and effectively and transforming the way we show up with one another. Donna Zajonc's beautiful book engages you early and connects you with the characters as they seek to apply The Empowerment Dynamic in profound ways. I will forever be inspired by the title's question, Who Do You Want to Be on the Way to What You Want?"

—**Julie Fox**, Vice President, Employee Engagement and Leadership Development, National Church Residences

. . . . . . . . . . .

"The Empowerment Dynamic has forever changed our organizational culture for the good. It has grounded and connected us through difficult business transitions. Perfectly timed, Donna Zajonc's new book will help all our people listen to and accept themselves, and more fully live from the heart."

—**Sheri Lawrence**, VP of Learning and Development, Studio Movie Grill

. . . . . . . . . . .

"Leaders MUST gain mastery over reactive tendencies so that we don't leave a wake of discouraged and disengaged people behind us. The story Donna shares with us illuminates the Dreaded Drama Triangle and The Empowerment Dynamic antidote roles of Coach, Creator, and Challenger, thereby showing us how to be better people and leaders. This book is a gem."

—**Dede Henley**, CEO, Henley Leadership Group; *Forbes* Contributor; Executive Coach

"Donna shows how to be a multi-dimensional coach supporting clients on the noble journey from Victim to Creator. Going beyond an either/or mindset, this book brings new insights and next-level results for individuals and teams seeking better outcomes."

—**Bert Parlee**, PhD, Psychologist, YPO/CFF Trainer

. . . . . . . . . . .

"I read this captivating book over the course of three days. Every time I sat down and opened it, I was able to accept the invitation to slow down in a way I only do when speaking with a great mentor or coach. I've never had that experience reading a book before. I will be giving this book to my colleagues for many years to come."

—**Diana Millies**, Director, Culture and Coaching, Frisenius Kidney Care

. . . . . . . . . . .

"Too often the focus is on performance, learning more and doing more, when what is most needed is a release from our habitual dramas. Donna Zajonc shows us how to do that in this compelling story of Sophia. A brilliant must-read for leaders as well as coaches."

—**Marita Fridjhon**, MSW, PSW, CPCC, CEO of CRR Global, co-author of *Creating Intelligent Teams: Leading with Relationship Systems Intelligence*

. . . . . . . . . . .

"Donna's new book is a game-changer for anyone who wants powerful coaching tips and tools to transform the Drama Triangle and step fully into their Creator essence. Never in the history of time has it been more important for people to awaken their Creator essence, and the profession of coaching has an illuminating and instrumental role to play. A must-read for our global profession and professionals."

—**Darren Robson**, Imagineer and Global Board Direction for the Association for Coaching

# Who Do You Want to Be

*On the Way to What You Want?*

Coaching with
The Empowerment Dynamic

# Who Do You Want to Be

*On the Way to What You Want?*

Coaching with
The Empowerment Dynamic

## Donna Zajonc, MCC

# Who Do You Want to Be
## *On the Way to What You Want?*

---

## Coaching with The Empowerment Dynamic

Published by

Polaris Publishing

321 High School Road NE—PMB 295

Bainbridge Island, WA 98110

Cover Design by
Shannon McCafferty

Interior Design by
Bob Lanphear

FIRST EDITION

ISBN: 9781733678100

*"So often in life, things that you regard as an impediment turn out to be great good fortune."*

—Ruth Bader Ginsburg
US Supreme Court Justice

# List of Diagrams

# Contents

# Foreword

I first met Donna Zajonc in the mid-2000s during my certification for The Leadership Circle Profile. Her husband, David Emerald, who had just released the book *The Power of TED* (*The Empowerment Dynamic)*, was serving as faculty for that workshop, held on beautiful Bainbridge Island, Washington. Combined with the leadership certification I had just completed, The Empowerment Dynamic practice was a perfect fit.

The Karpman Drama Triangle*, nicknamed by David as the "Dreaded Drama Triangle," or "DDT," instantly illuminates patterns of behavior that limit a person's potential for full creative leadership. Once you see drama described using that model, it's hard to unsee. The DDT's positive counterpart, TED* (*The Empowerment Dynamic), as I've used it in my work with the Leadership Circle, interrupts the "drama dance" of our automatic reactive tendencies by raising our awareness of roles and patterns we are adopting that are actually preventing us from getting

---

*The Karpman Drama Triangle is a social model of human interaction first described by Dr. Stephen B. Karpman in the late 1960s. The triangle maps a type of destructive interaction that can emerge in relationship conflict, involving three actors in the drama: Victim, Persecutor and Rescuer.

what we want. In one-on-one work as well as with teams and departments, I've repeatedly witnessed the big shift that takes place when I introduce The Empowerment Dynamic into the mix. Practicing such "pattern awareness" and getting curious about it is the golden ticket to transforming destructive patterns and unlocking our creative potential.

When Donna asked if I would write the foreword, I was deeply honored because I have such respect for Donna and for The Empowerment Dynamic frameworks that she and her husband, David, have co-created.

As one of Donna's co-facilitators in her coaching course, I have always appreciated her deep personal practice of this work and the way she leads in the world. Donna has led a life dedicated to service, helping others find their way, offering tools for those times when help is most needed. She has an inherent belief in humanity, in awakening each person's potential, and in advocating for those who aren't able to advocate for themselves.

In her original education and practice as a mental health nurse, Donna saw the need for certain changes in the mental health system. Rather than merely resent what was lacking, she moved into politics to make a difference in that system from a policy perspective and by inspiring collective action. Along the way, she found coaching—not only found it, but mastered it and became a Master Certified Coach through the International Coaching Federation. She has a keenly developed ability to activate someone's creative curiosity, helping them to uncover unexplored avenues of possibility.

This work of transitioning from the drama roles of the DDT to the creative, empowering roles of TED*

(*The Empowerment Dynamic) is easy to understand and "see." It is a simple yet profound formula we can use to begin to change our brain's wiring and our patterns of negative behavior by asking straightforward questions. I've used it repeatedly with my clients and they "get it" in an instant as their patterns are clearly revealed. But the work that follows isn't always so easy. It must become a practice.

I am grateful to Donna for writing this book—a story of the ever-evolving practice of a Master Coach. As someone who often finds DDT patterns running almost undetectably in my mental background noise, I appreciate the subtlety of practice this story teaches and evokes.

As her co-facilitator, I've seen how Donna takes this work to heart, consistently raising her awareness of the DDT and shifting to The Empowerment Dynamic. Using her own dramas as her petri dish, she has advanced the very frameworks she teaches. A natural systems thinker, Donna saw broader applications of this work, making inroads to help people access it at even deeper levels to unlock the traps we humans so consistently, if unwittingly, seem to set for ourselves.

I'm excited that this book has found its way to you. In reading it, you are likely to feel seen and understood in ways that may surprise you. Reading about the inner struggles and insights of the characters you meet here, you may recognize your own. You'll see how, when we are inspired to listen, reflect, and choose our way out of our damaging DDT cycles, self-compassion becomes our guide.

This work of moving out of drama toward empowerment is a dance that integrates human life with its spiritual foundation. I'm excited that you're about to spend time with this story that unfolds new aspects of The Empowerment Dynamic. Enjoy, and let your own story unfold.

Amy Felix-Reese
*Senior Vice President, Client Services*
**Full Circle Group** and **The Leadership Circle**
Boulder, Colorado

# Introduction

On the dashboard of your car, you notice a flashing red light that signals that something serious is happening under the hood. You are grateful for the red light because it's a chance to check the owner's manual, learn more about how your car operates, and ask for help if you need additional support. You could also choose to ignore the conspicuous red light and continue driving as if nothing is wrong. Pretty soon you are oblivious to that warning light flashing, while your car's engine runs dangerously hot.

This metaphor illustrates our current challenge as human beings. Will we notice the flashing red lights that are trying to get our attention about the way we live and relate to each other? When our personal habits are at stake, it is common to want to ignore the warning signs and protect what is familiar. Yet whatever we resist, we give energy to, causing it to expand and grow. Why not remove the power we give to the parts of ourselves we tend to reject and keep hidden? Instead, we could choose to accept the challenge—to bring these troublemakers to the surface of our consciousness and welcome them as part of our transformational journey.

Sophia, the main character in this story, is on just such a journey. Deeply concerned for the state of the world, she longs to make a meaningful contribution. While the details are different, Sophia's story is my story. Early in my career, I was a community mental health nurse who became concerned about our public health policy. Hoping to effect change through elected service, I ran for, and won, a seat in the Oregon legislature. I spent ten years in partisan politics, serving in office and managing political campaigns. After leaving public life, I shifted my focus to personal and spiritual growth, which led me to discover professional coaching. When I became certified as a coach over twenty years ago, I aspired to partner with others who wanted to become more conscious of their own inner and emotional lives—people committed to working together toward solutions to the pressing issues facing humanity and our planet.

What coaching helped me discover was how easy it had been to suppress the parts of myself that I didn't want to see, for fear of what I might discover. I learned that, in the real (not imaginary) process of human transformation, ignoring my negative habits and troubling emotions wasn't going to be an option.

David Emerald, who has played so many roles in my life—friend, colleague, husband, and teacher, wrote *The Power of TED* * (*The Empowerment Dynamic)* over fifteen years ago. In his book, David drew upon his own journey of getting stuck in the Drama Triangle roles of Victim, Persecutor, and Rescuer. Tired of being stuck, he asked the God of his understanding, "I am ready to surrender my Victim stance in the world, but

I need to know: What is the opposite of a Victim?" David's immediate insight was that the opposite of a Victim is a Creator. Starting with the role of Creator, he worked out an antidote to the Dreaded Drama Triangle (DDT for short, like the poison). That antidote triangle became TED* (*The Empowerment Dynamic), with its positive roles of Creator, Challenger, and Coach.

Together David and I expanded our consulting, facilitation, and coaching business based on The Empowerment Dynamic frameworks. As we focused on sharing the frameworks with others, we deepened our personal understanding of the power of this work. We began to hear similar questions in our training and coaching sessions:

- *Why do the same drama roles keep reappearing in my life?*

- *Now that I know about the Dreaded Drama Triangle, why am I still getting stuck in the drama?*

- *How do I stop myself from going into the DDT in the first place?*

- And the all-time favorite: *How can I get others to shift out of the DDT and into TED*?*

Fascinated by these questions, I continued to investigate the origins of our patterns of human drama. David and I developed unique exercises and trainings that supported participants in catching their DDT patterns sooner so they could transform them more quickly and easily. But as I considered my role in sharing this work with others, my internal Persecutor voice grew louder and stronger. As someone who still often found myself trapped in the DDT, how could I teach this material? Wouldn't I be exposed as a fraud? Before long I concluded that, as a co-author of these tools and frameworks, I should be able to *perfectly* avoid getting caught in the DDT! It's laughable now, but at the time, this harsh internal message sounded extremely convincing.

As I began meditating, journaling, and learning the importance of self-care, I became more aware of my Inner Persecutor. I saw how I placed constant pressure on myself, as if I alone were responsible for fixing the world's problems. Most of all, I wanted to fix myself—there seemed to be quite a lot wrong with me! With time, however, and with more self-compassion, I eased up on myself. And at that point, a new series of questions emerged: *How do I learn from these drama patterns, rather than push them away? How can my reactive patterns show me the way to being the person I want to be? How can I best teach and coach others how to share this work? Who do I want to be . . . on the way to what I want?*

Reflecting on these questions, I began concentrating my focus on observing my inner life. By staying open to learning, I discovered it was possible to make friends with my "Inner DDT." I could just watch its antics without judgment. Doing this became a way to nurture my true self to emerge in the TED* roles of Creator, Challenger, and Coach. The more I listened to my internal self-talk, the more obvious it became that the relationship I had with *myself* had been guiding the way I related to others, and to life in general.

A whole new approach to working with my active inner dialogue began to emerge for me, and with it, the path to an empowered relationship with the outside world. It became clear that my personal transformation was an inside-out process. It started with awakening my inner observer and continued with a consistent curiosity—a desire to understand all the different parts of myself—even the ones I had been avoiding or denying.

This epiphany revealed I had been treating my drama like a movie streaming on a flat-screen TV or computer. If I don't like the movie, I can turn it off, right? But then, isn't the movie still streaming? Of course it is! I might try to ignore my life story—all my dramas, beliefs, and struggles—but they would still go on streaming just beneath my conscious awareness. I could choose to turn off the movie, turn away from the drama, or keep watching to discover how it was getting me hooked.

With the publication of David's second book, *3 Vital Questions: Transforming Workplace Drama*, the 3 Vital Questions (3VQ) became a practical way for individuals, teams, and entire organizations to work together in powerfully collaborative ways, often with the support of professional coaching. Our trainings and our community of certified trainers expanded exponentially.

It was then that I began to focus on professional coaching and the ways in which coaches might be more effective by applying The Empowerment Dynamic and 3VQ. At the same time, I heard a plea from my organizational clients: They wanted to be more "coach-like" in the way they communicated and in the way they led at work and home. The idea for this book began to evolve.

If you're familiar with David's teaching story, *The Power of TED\**, you will recognize the main character in this book: Sophia, the coach who walks with Ted and David. In this new story, we look in on Sophia many years later, after she has become an experienced professional coach. You will hear Sophia's internal dialogue, her doubts and worries, as she learns to quiet her mind in service of coaching a headstrong client. The coaching dialogue here reveals tools and methods intended to help you coach and empower yourself as well as others. And you will discover that you do not need to be a professional coach to learn to be more "coach-like." This book has one purpose: to support those who wish to become the best version of themselves they can be.

As we honor all parts of ourselves, we open a doorway: the power to choose. But not everyone wants to walk through that door. In fact, some clients protest: *How dare you show me that doorway?!* We often sense that what lies just beneath our awareness will bring up pain and fear. So, when problems arise, and they always do, we may default to revving up the old drama habits, digging in, and getting defensive. Continually choosing this cycle of avoidance, we develop fixed ideas of who we are or should be, how the world should be, and even who others should be. We lose our inquisitiveness and stunt our curiosity. Locked in that cycle, the creative energy we need for positive change is hard to come by. Drama then dominates not just our minds, but our home, work, and school environments.

Drama and its poisons can spread through entire cultures habituated to avoiding the truth of collective, systemic patterns. Turning away from our pain and fear, we unwittingly enable the deep polarizations that have now characterized our social discourse for many decades, worldwide.

But there is an alternative to fueling our fears and limiting our self-awareness. When we notice our drama and reactive habits, when we name and explore them, we create the opportunity to have a warmer relationship with those parts of ourselves. With some support and a few helpful pointers along the way, we learn to treat ourselves as we would treat a good friend. Seeing our drama roles as gifts of awakening, we can recognize our armor as the heavy burden it is, set it down, and see clearly that it is not who we are.

This is the journey, the road to authenticity: embracing the totality of our experience, including our dramas. We can become adept at recognizing when we are caught in the undertow of emotional reactivity. Instead of being our enemies or worst nightmares, our drama patterns and the emotions they evoke become our natural guidance system—far more effective when we pay attention to its flashing red warning lights!

But however skillfully we may navigate, life will bring storms that throw our readings off. Recently, my most intimate relations have been full of changes and challenges. I became a new grandmother just three weeks after my own mother passed. My immediate family has experienced loss of work, a mental health crisis, and healing and recovery from alcoholism, all against the backdrop of immense loss and grief due to a pandemic, the collective trauma of systemic racism, economic disparity, attacks on the US Capitol, and an escalating climate crisis. Yet even in the face of all this, I know that our natural wisdom and intelligence are always available to us. We have the power to address these challenges. As long as we don't run away from the parts of ourselves we would rather hide—if we heed their warnings and shift our focus to what needs our attention—our wisest and best selves will show up to meet the moment.

The pandemic has magnified and brought to light the many aspects of life on Earth that need our immediate attention. Central to addressing each of these important issues is *how we relate to one another.* Our very lives as global citizens depend on our learning to connect more deeply, to listen to and trust one another so that we can effectively work together toward innovative solutions to our shared problems.

I began writing this book as the Covid-19 pandemic began to unfold. Since then, our lives have been reshaped in untold ways. I chose, however, not to include the pandemic in the setting of this story. The characters are unmasked, and they shake hands, share hugs, and at times walk arm in arm. I decided there was enough drama in life to illustrate the points I am teaching without adding the dilemmas presented by the pandemic!

There is an important note to make here. As a former mental health nurse, I am very much aware that coaching with The Empowerment Dynamic cannot act as substitute for psychotherapy or psychiatry. Some of us have experienced deep traumas that make it essential to seek the support of knowledgeable professionals who are experienced in healing such trauma and guiding its recovery. If you recognize yourself in this description, please do not hesitate to ask for professional support.

It is often said that history judges a generation based upon the questions its people asked. In the future, others will study this time in our history and take note of what we asked of ourselves. Did we ask how we could disentangle ourselves from outdated reactive, drama-filled habits that threatened to keep us from knowing our true nature as wise and caring human beings? Did we work to quiet our obsessive distractions in order to consider the needs of others? Did we acknowledge that all beings everywhere and all cultures have the same innate intelligence, the same heart of basic goodness? Did we take individual and collective responsibility, and then did we take action to find solutions that help and respect all people while supporting the Earth itself to thrive?

My hope is that the story you are about to read will support you in embracing your best self, and that it will encourage you to become a fearless activist for your personal transformation. For as we release ourselves from the grip of our habitual dramas, little by little we are transforming ourselves—and simultaneously changing the world.

Donna Zajonc, MCC
**Center for The Empowerment Dynamic**
Bainbridge Island, Washington, USA
September 2021

# 1

## An Intriguing Opportunity

D ang. It's the second night this week I'm awake at 2:45."

Sophia sank into the corner of her couch with a cluster of soft pillows tucked around her, still half asleep. She wiggled back and forth trying to get comfortable and sank deeper into the couch. Suddenly remembering she had a cup of hot mint tea in her right hand, she rebalanced her body again, trying to get comfortable.

Sophia placed her cup on the coffee table and brushed a few drops of tea from the leg of her flannel pajamas. As she leaned forward, she noticed the tall stack of books—some she had read and many she had not. Some days she felt she personally kept the book industry afloat with her book-buying habit. She picked up the teacup and raised it to her lips. Taking a slow, deep inhale of the minty fragrance, she reached for the paper at the top of her waiting-to-read stack, wondering if she was the only one left in her neighborhood who still took the newspaper. Holding the Sunday paper in her hands and reading it from cover to cover remained one of her favorite small joys in life.

The full moon shone brightly through the living room picture window. Sophia looked at her colorful flowerpots on her front porch. One of the good things about leaving her corporate coaching job was no more downtown office, no wild commute. "I wouldn't trade my home office for anything now," she thought. "My leadership coaching business is flourishing just fine from my home and I still have time to nurture the flowers and small yard I enjoy so much." While working full time, her generous salary had allowed her to take advantage of low interest rates and refinance her Pacific Northwest home. For the first time since her divorce, Sophia felt a sense of financial security.

Sophia looked past her stack of books and caught sight of the colorful photo collage sitting atop the coffee table. She liked the cute picture in the middle of her only child, her son Gabe, at age seven in his fishing gear, standing in the boat, holding up his first catch. But her favorite was the one of Gabe at his high school graduation, jauntily sporting his cap and gown and grinning from ear to ear.

"We were so close," Sophia remembered. "Little did I know then that Gabe would move thousands of miles away and I wouldn't see him often. He is a young man finding his way in the world, but I do miss him."

Having recently celebrated a "decade birthday," Sophia now felt the end of her life was nearer than its beginning. That birthday milestone had gotten her attention. More profound and frequent questions were emerging about what mattered most to her. What unique gifts and values did she have that could be honed further? Was she doing all she could to become a bold voice for positive change? Where was she finding meaning and joy?

Two things usually helped Sophia go back to sleep when she experienced wakeful nights like this one. A mug of her favorite mint tea, cupped in her hands, and writing in her journal. Something about getting those recurring thoughts out of her head and onto the page helped calm her mind. She reached for her journal in its special spot on the coffee table and took out her pen.

Sophia had always enjoyed personal reflection. She tended to look for silver linings rather than focusing on negativity or problems, though sometimes she wondered if that was the best way to be. She lowered her pen to the page and began to write. *I've been kind of stuck in believing that just thinking positively is all I need to do. But so many questions are coming up for me now. I can't deny I'm feeling confused.*

She knew that tomorrow morning she would pay a price for this middle-of-the-night journaling session. "But I do love this silence, even though my mind is racing," she thought. She continued writing: *Whatever time I have left on earth, I want to spend it wisely. Are my thoughts and actions moving me closer to being who I want to be? In the end, it is really about accountability, about choosing the person I want to be and what contribution I want to make in the world, right here, right now.*

Mulling over what she had just written, Sophia took in a deep breath and let it out with a sigh. The refrigerator motor switched on, and she jumped a little. "Guess I'm a bit on edge," she thought.

Sophia continued writing: *How do I transform what is off balance when I am not sure what is bothering me? How do I get clarity about what matters most to me?*

The nighttime silence seemed to grow heavy. Something was wrong. "But what?" she thought. "What is keeping me up in the middle of the night?"

In that moment, as if in answer, Sophia saw in her mind's eye the company president, who a few years earlier had hired her to create what he called "a people-centered culture." He had wooed her with a generous budget and a coach's dream—a full year to develop and plan an all-new company coaching program. He had promised her all the support she would need for a multi-year commitment.

"This is my ideal client," she remembered telling herself. "I've finally found my place and an opportunity to be the bold coach and change agent I want to be." She felt such hope and gratitude that her longing to make a meaningful contribution in the world would finally be realized.

She had made several trips that year to the beach retreat where her mentor Ted lived. Together they had gotten inspired, putting the finishing details on the new Leader as Coach Empowerment Program. When she presented the elements of the plan to the company president, he enthusiastically praised her approach, saying he wanted to highlight the new program at the upcoming annual meeting and to start preparing the materials and specifics she needed to make it a success. The night before the annual meeting, Sophia had hardly slept, she was so excited. She had stayed up putting the finishing touches on her presentation script and video. She had never worked so hard or put so much of her heart and soul into a project.

The next morning the auditorium had been abuzz, full of her co-workers and company employees. She had coped well with a bad case of butterflies as she eagerly waited for the program to start and her time on the agenda.

Just minutes before it was time to walk up the back stairs to the stage, the company vice president, George, pulled her aside. "Things have changed, Sophia," he whispered, frowning. "The president and I have decided to go a different direction. In a few minutes he will announce a change in the company's budget priorities. We are redirecting your budget for the coaching program to the new product research team. We believe there is an economic downturn coming, so the company can't afford your program anymore. Sorry for the late notice, but the decision is final. He asked me to relay the information to you since he didn't have time to talk with you before today. You can still sit on the stage with us, though, if you wish, but you are off the agenda."

There are brief moments in life that seem surreal—a thick, dark void that folds over itself, both real and unreal in the same instant. This was one of those time-stopping moments.

Stunned, Sophia stammered, trying to find words that could possibly make a difference. "But . . . wait . . . this can't be true." But the vice president had already started walking up the stairs, onto the stage, and was sitting down next to the president.

She stood in the hallway and felt a gripping anger rise, gathering intensity and power with each second.

"There's no way in hell I am sitting on that stage, acting like nothing has happened," she declared to herself.

She felt embarrassed, invisible, and heartbroken. A year's worth of work and an opportunity to implement the best work she had ever designed, and with Ted, no less, had vanished in an instant. But that hadn't been the most hurtful part. As the days wore on, she felt the grief of a personal and professional rejection by someone who didn't live the values and behaviors he said he wanted for his company culture.

She understood a company needs to be profitable and make difficult decisions. Sophia's anger had stemmed from outrage at the president's lack of courage to have an authentic conversation with her about his plan to scrap the project. She had invested her heart and soul into a leader that espoused a vision of a human-centered, collaborative culture but did not live it himself.

The morning after the annual meeting, Sophia put her letter of immediate resignation on the president's desk. Technically she wasn't fired, but in her mind that was how she thought it. On the drive home, with her hands clenching the steering wheel, she had vowed she would never again work with a leader who lacked accountability, who hadn't committed to "walk their talk" and live aligned with the values they championed. Sophia had promised herself then and there that she would accept only clients who pledged to do their personal work first, before they asked their staff or anyone else to do theirs.

None of the situation had been her fault, she told herself. She was powerless and felt like a victim of the situation. Over time she reflected many times about the "incident" and often asked herself, "How did I misjudge that situation so badly? Did my intense desire to be of service prevent me from picking up on the truth about the realities of that company culture?" She felt powerless to what happened to her while also blaming herself for not having a clearer crystal ball.

Sophia took another sip of tea. "Amazing how vivid it all is, after all this time!" she thought. "I guess what's bothering me right now, though, is that somehow I don't trust myself. Like maybe I won't stay true to my promises and the personal changes I've said I am committed to." In the deep darkness of midnight, she heard her critical inner voice that was quick to blame herself when things went wrong.

Now she saw what had been keeping her up at 2:45 a.m. "What if another exciting project comes along from an influential company, promising to invest in their people and culture but it's really all smoke and mirrors? Will I take it just for the income and succumb to my need to please with a quick yes? Or will I stick to the vow I made to myself—to work only with the willing—those leaders who are committed to doing the hard work of personal transformation?"

A week earlier, Sophia had received an email from the CEO of an influential construction company whose national headquarters was nearby. The CEO wanted to meet Sophia and talk about the possibility of hiring her to lead a company-wide training project. Sophia was well acquainted with RJ Construction, a company whose name was on the local sports stadium and graced the sides of dozens of city buses. The famed business had been run by the CEO's father and grandfather for the better part of three generations—a family business run by its founders. And now the daughter and granddaughter of the founders sat at the helm. If the business write-ups were to be believed, she did not suffer fools and had a reputation for being strong-willed and difficult to work for. Sophia was curious about this strong woman leader who had claimed a top position in an industry traditionally ruled by men.

Despite her curiosity, Sophia instantly thought, "I'm already working more hours than I want, plus I do not want to risk another disappointment. A new training project with a client I don't know—it just isn't in the cards right now." But instead of the "Thanks, but no thanks" email she intended to write, Sophia found herself writing a courteous reply saying she would be glad to meet the CEO and hear about the project.

As soon as she had hit Send and heard the email swoosh away, Sophia felt that uneasy pang of her strong drive to work hard and keep pressing, always saying yes. As she thought more about it, it wasn't that she didn't have time for a new client. There was something else, a nagging inward tug. And now here she was, wide awake, still wondering about it.

"Why did I say yes to meeting her? Am I doing this just for the money and status of working with a prominent company? Am I fearful of working with another leader that doesn't walk their talk? Or am I scared I won't walk my talk?"

She sipped her tea. In the quiet she heard a familiar, tender voice speaking from within. It spoke clearly, without judgment. "Stay true to your commitments," she heard loud and clear.

Sophia cupped her mug. Its warmth comforted her as she gazed out at the dark, peaceful room. Sophia had heard that voice before. Sometimes she followed its wise guidance and at other times she kept busy and pretended not to hear it.

After a while, she took up her pen and wrote, *When I focus too intensely on work, keep a ridiculously busy schedule, and don't take care of myself, I let my need to please take over. When I do this, I don't have room or attention for my authentic inner voice. Am I doing that now? Is my urge to contribute in a big way overshadowing what is best for me personally?*

There it was—her core fear. She had been betrayed and disrespected by that company president and was scared that her desire to please and be of service, at the expense of what was good for herself, would result in another devastating disappointment. It was that simple.

"I've lived with this clash of identities all of my life, haven't I?" Sophia thought. "Outwardly I am confident, calm, poised, and competent. Inwardly I am self-critical and doubt myself, devaluing my own self-care while wondering if I will ever find a place where I can make the contribution I long to make."

A drizzle of cold tea trickled down her arm, pulling her attention back to the moment.

"Whoops!" She reached to mop up the splash of tea with a napkin.

"Hey," she thought, "Where am I putting my focus right now? Am I focusing on my fears and not trusting myself? Am I focusing on my internal doubts? That's what I *don't* want."

Just then that wise inner voice she heard earlier spoke up again. "What is it that I *do* want?" she said aloud.

The strength of her voice surprised her a little. Almost immediately, Sophia felt the power of that question. It seemed almost to vibrate throughout her body. Just noticing and naming that she was stuck on what she didn't want helped calm her fearful thoughts. Her shoulders relaxed. She drew in a long, deep belly breath.

In taking just those few moments to pause, Sophia's mind began to settle, and she could feel her inner wisdom rising. "I trust myself to not be overly eager and show up as a pleaser and overachiever, looking for the next great project that will make my life feel worthwhile. I trust myself to listen, take it slow, and live in alignment with my values," she affirmed to herself. "My job is to follow the ocean of inner wisdom that is inside me. That is my focus and my desired outcome. That is what *I do* want."

She smiled as she took up her pen and wrote.

*I am judging this CEO and her company by reputation alone. Whatever biases and fears I have, I can let them go for now. I will suspend judgment and listen and stay open to possibilities. I will keep my commitment to myself that I will work only with leaders who want to engage in their own personal transformation. Leaders must do their own personal work first before they ask anyone else to do theirs.*

"That one's not up for negotiation," she affirmed, then wrote, *I trust myself to show up authentically for this client conversation.*

Sophia set down her journal and strolled to the kitchen. She washed her mug, set it on the drainboard, and turned out the light.

# 2

## Taming a Trigger

A s expected, Sophia's rough night made it harder to wake up. This morning she opted for a cup of coffee rather than her usual tea. The discomfort she felt during the wee hours had begun to settle.

The microwave dinged and signaled that her bagel was warm. As she was finishing the bagel and cream cheese a little while later, she heard a chime from her phone, signaling she had a text. The assistant to the CEO with whom she had an appointment later that morning had texted Sophia that the CEO was "very busy," adding that her appointment would be one of several back-to-back meetings that morning. The assistant's text ended saying she hoped Sophia "would not be late so that your time with RJ won't be cut short."

Sophia frowned and arched her back. A tight ball gathered in her gut like a clenching fist, and her mind suddenly turned critical. "I'm not a child! I don't need to be told to be on time," she grumbled. "What kind of CEO expects their assistant to tell clients not to be late? Good grief!" Downing the rest of her coffee, Sophia set her mug down on the counter and paused for a moment to get curious about her anger.

She cringed. "How does this happen?" she thought. "One little text message and I'm triggered. My critical, judging mind erupts!" She shook her head as she gathered her things to leave. "All my serenity, gone with a single text."

Her good friend and mentor Ted taught her that if she could pay attention to what triggered her, she would discover potent insights into what she cared about. Pausing and getting curious about the situation or person that got her triggered would increase her self-awareness. Ted frequently reminded her of this point and tutored her to treat a triggering moment as a secret gift, ready to be unwrapped.

It had been over fifteen years since Sophia first met Ted. She had rented a beach cottage to recover and heal after the loss of her marriage. Through a serendipitous meeting on the beach one evening, she had met a friend of Ted's who later suggested the two of them should meet.

She paused now to gaze out her kitchen window. A hummingbird was hovering there, suckling on a bright yellow daylily. "That first week of walking on the beach with Ted, reflecting and healing and learning about the Karpman Drama Triangle and, of course, The Empowerment Dynamic, changed my life," she recalled.

On their walks, Ted shared his insights about the Karpman Drama Triangle, a diagram he had playfully renamed the "Dreaded Drama Triangle," or DDT, as he called it, and its three roles of Victim, Persecutor, and Rescuer. As Sophia listened and walked with him that week, life seemed to make sense in ways she had never experienced before.

Along with that, Ted presented Sophia a new and ingenious positive *alternative* triangle—one he had named TED* or *The Empowerment Dynamic, which served as an antidote to the DDT. With a childlike chuckle and smile, he insisted to Sophia that the diagram's name was pure coincidence.

From their first meeting, Sophia was immediately taken with Ted's insights, his openness to share his personal stories, and most of all, his sense of humor. Ted was nearly fifteen years her senior, and yet something about him was ageless. The two stayed in touch, and Sophia soon found that Ted always seemed to have a helpful word or a strategic insight that could help her solve even the stickiest dilemma.

Sophia sought Ted's counsel when the coaching program they spent a year designing was suddenly cancelled. She felt like a Victim to the president's hasty decision and poor communication. She had been so sure the new Leader as Coach Empowerment Program would be a huge success. This was the contribution she longed to make—to partner with others to help them be their best self and make a positive impact in the world.

Sophia welcomed the chance to hear Ted's wisdom about dealing with disappointment, and she wanted him to help her understand why she felt so hopeless. He had worked as diligently as she had on that program, always ready with enthusiastic suggestions, visibly pleased to help her clarify her vision. And yet when it had fallen through, he had laughed—a big belly laugh. "The more things change, the more they stay the same!" Ted had managed to make her smile even as she delivered what she had thought was the worst possible news.

Year by year, their collaborative dialogues had set Sophia on a path of lifelong learning.

"How did Ted describe a trigger?" she now mused. "Ah yes," she recalled, "When you get triggered, it means you're having an exaggerated response to something happening in the moment. It means there's something you want or need that is blocked or thwarted. Ted said that if I pay close attention, I will get clues to what is happening, and he said to then pause and listen to what I can learn."

"Right." Sophia smiled. "If I notice what got me triggered in the first place, I can learn what my strong reaction is trying to tell me." Just by hanging out with Ted, she had learned to appreciate her triggers. They were leading her out of drama patterns and toward learning new levels of awareness.

"So what about the assistant's text got me so triggered?" she asked herself. Sophia looked up and turned her gaze across the kitchen, focusing on nothing in particular as she noticed her breath rising and lowering. "I want to feel respected. I interpreted that text as disrespecting my ability to be on time."

She was distracted out of her reverie by an alert from a business app. Someone had just invited Sophia to join their network. Consciously shifting her attention back to the assistant's text and her own reflective thoughts, she sensed how on edge she was about meeting the CEO. The assistant's text had triggered her worry all over again.

She closed her eyes and took three deep breaths. As she took in the cool air, Sophia remembered her commitment: "I focus on what I want, not on what

I *don't* want." Then, with intention, she reaffirmed, "I acknowledge my judgments about RJ and her construction company, and I let them go. I trust myself to listen to what she has to say while remaining open to possibilities."

Just as Ted had promised, once Sophia acknowledged her triggers rather than suppressing them, she never failed to gain some insight into what had caused her to get triggered in the first place. "There's no need to judge RJ's assistant or take her text personally. She's just trying to do her job," she thought. She felt the tightness of that judgment fall away and a degree of calm return to her body. "Ahh. Now I'm ready for that meeting!"

On the drive into the city, new doubts cropped up. "Will there be an authentic connection with this CEO? Can I trust her?" She began to imagine what working for this company would be like. As those thoughts gained momentum, she remembered the metaphor she had learned on her meditation retreat, of watching her thoughts as though she were sitting in a theater viewing a movie. It helped her to get distance from her reactive thoughts and judgments. "I'm going to use this commute time to relax rather than ruminate on my judgments," she thought. She turned on the soft jazz radio station and listened to music for the rest of the drive.

RJ Construction's corporate office reception area had a traditional feel, with a big leather couch. Two club chairs flanked a coffee table that was sporting professional photo books titled *RJ Construction Homes*. Off to one side was a tabletop 3D architectural model of a dozen homes, illustrating a neighborhood plan. On the wall hung two large framed posters of the company's award-winning home designs.

As she browsed the big room, she came to two larger-than-life portraits. "The founders of RJ Construction, I'll bet," she mused. Engraved brass plates affixed to the frames announced that the gray-haired man in a dark three-piece suit was "RJ Senior" and that the man wearing a crisp work shirt and sport coat was "RJ Junior."

"Definitely a family-run business!" she thought.

As an office door opened, Sophia saw that it had a brass plate engraved with "CEO." A blonde woman in her late forties emerged and strode into the waiting room wearing a crisp blue button-down shirt, the pocket embroidered with the cursive *RJ* of the company logo. In dark designer jeans and stylish shoes, she projected a relaxed confidence.

"You must be Sophia. I'm RJ. Happy you could make time today. Please come in," she said, motioning toward her office. RJ's greeting—her kind smile and direct eye contact—made a good first impression.

RJ held the door for Sophia and pointed to a comfortable leather chair in front of a magnificent desk made of hand-polished Northwest timber. "If that desk is supposed to be impressive, it's sure working," thought Sophia. "It must be more than a hundred years old."

As RJ walked around the desk to take her seat, Sophia noticed a tall glass sculpture at one end. Its base read, "Rotarian of the Year." The rest of the desktop was covered with architectural prints and notes, a few stacks of business cards, and a scattered assortment of invoices.

Sophia wondered if the collection of papers on RJ's desk was a result of her busy schedule or a disorganized mind. "Maybe it's both," she thought.

"I'm really pleased to meet you, Sophia," RJ said. "You come highly recommended by more than one of my trusted associates. They all agree you're a great coach and trainer. I don't know what I need exactly, but I know the company needs some help. I'm anxious to get your advice."

Sophia nodded and smiled. "Thank you, I'm happy to be here. Tell me a little more about your company."

"Sure. RJ Construction is named after my grandfather, Richard James, RJ Senior. He started working in construction over seventy-five years ago. Maybe you saw his picture in our waiting room. From the time he was a young boy everyone called him RJ, hence the name RJ Construction. My dad, RJ Junior, spent his life alongside Grandpa, growing this construction company into what it is now. Today we specialize in neighborhood developments and employ hundreds of people across the country.

"It was no secret that my dad wanted a son to help him carry on the business." RJ laughed. "But as it turned out, Mom and Dad had two girls. Being the eldest, I inherited the RJ legacy. My given name is Regina Jo, but in junior high I told everyone my name was RJ and it stuck. So now I'm RJ Number Three." She smiled softly, then looked down for a moment, turning serious.

"My dad died suddenly of a heart attack at just fifty-two. My mom and the team kept things going, but she really had no interest in the business. So right after college, I stepped in. That was almost twenty-five years ago."

"That's quite a history," said Sophia. "Looks like you and your family have created a very successful business here."

"Well, yes and no. Depends on what you call successful. We're profitable all right, and we manage to survive, even thrive, during the ups and downs in the economy," said RJ. "But I asked to see you because I just saw the results of our annual company survey, and it's obvious that some of my employees definitely would not rate RJ Construction a success.

"The employee engagement scores are really low, well below industry standard, but it is the awful trust scores that surprised me the most. In the comments section, one of the most frequent criticisms was that our employees don't feel comfortable speaking up or taking risks. I've seen similar comments in previous surveys, but this time they were even worse. We must be doing something wrong," RJ said. "It looks like a lot of our employees don't like working here."

Sophia nodded with an understanding gesture, then felt a strong urge to ask a few questions. She wanted to show RJ she was a competent professional, but instead of talking, Sophia paused, took a deep breath, and trusted her intuition to remain silent. She sensed RJ had more to share.

"I know these issues didn't just pop up overnight," RJ continued. "I inherited a very traditional way of doing things. Since the beginning, it was my grandpa or my dad who made all the decisions, and everyone just followed their lead. They owned the company after all; their name was on the door. Nobody questioned them or made suggestions, even when another approach might have been warranted. And I've tried my best to follow in their footsteps, you know, and carry on the family tradition. I thought that meant running things the way my dad and grandpa did.

"I wasn't conscious of it when I started out, but now I think I had the idea that my job was to keep a 'tough guy' image. Projecting 'I know best' was the only way I'd ever seen my dad and grandfather run RJ Construction. Taking over as a young woman right out of college, I didn't want to mess up, so I tried to carry on like I thought they would want me to.

"And to be honest," RJ admitted, "the economy was going so well when I took over that even the worst manager would have made money building homes.

"I guess what I realized reading these survey results is that, even after twenty-five years, I still question whether I know what I'm doing. I am really good at projecting strength and the know-how that keep this huge company running, but if I stop for even a second, I wonder if I know as much as I think I do."

RJ had been looking directly at Sophia as she spoke, but after her last comment she seemed uncomfortable and looked down at her hands resting on the desk. Sophia noticed she was twirling a ring on her right hand and felt RJ's confident persona wilt.

"It must be lonely for RJ," Sophia thought, "trying to keep up a 'tough guy' family business, never having had the mentoring she needed. This may be the first true glimpse for her of a new possibility—to lead the company in her own unique, creative way." She smiled and waited to see if RJ would say more.

After a pregnant pause RJ looked up again. "Anyway, I know our company needs some help, maybe a new company initiative about leadership or something, and maybe some coaching for people on our leadership team. I don't really know. Maybe I am the one who needs help!" She laughed, a little too awkwardly. "I'm the CEO of this outfit. The buck stops here, right?"

Sophia did a quick run-through in her own mind. There was so much going on with RJ and the poor company scores she hardly knew where to start. Sophia silently reminded herself, "Stay present, do not overpromise or try to please RJ with an inauthentic glossing over of the issues. Say what you are feeling."

"Thank you for your vulnerability and openness, RJ. It sounds like the company survey has given you quite a lot to think about. What would you say is bothering you the most . . . right now?" Sophia was genuinely curious about what RJ would say.

RJ looked off into the distance, collecting her thoughts. "What bothers me most . . . ?" she echoed. Sophia could see RJ taking deep breaths and her chest rising in response. It looked like RJ was reviewing a long list in her mind and couldn't decide which item bothered her the most.

"Well, on the surface it's these terrible employee scores. I like to be successful and when I see such low scores . . . well . . . it's really uncomfortable and I can't deny the numbers. That bothers me," she said.

"I can understand they bother you, and I appreciate that is what prompted you to call me. What is bothering you personally, RJ, about your life here as the CEO?"

RJ nodded her head slowly like she was still deciding what to say. "I know I need people to bring their ideas and their creativity, but I don't know how to get them to do it. I tell them that's what I want. But when I point out what's wrong with an idea, I can see it makes them mad. I guess I'm apt to criticize unfamiliar approaches." She sighed.

"I used to think I was a natural leader," RJ said slowly. "But now, I'm not so sure. We're still putting up billboard ads all over town with my name and face on them, big as day. It puts a lot of pressure on me to be the face and power behind this company. I don't really want the company to be all about me. I mean, I like running this show, but . . . I'm really tired.

"What bothers me most?" RJ restated. "It bothers me that all the responsibility is on my shoulders—that I have to constantly push and stay on top of everything to keep this company profitable. I just don't know who will do it if I don't," she confessed.

RJ's assistant knocked at the door, then opened it slightly and announced, "Frank is here from the bank. What should I tell him?"

"This is it. The next appointment," thought Sophia, reaching for her bag, preparing to leave. Sophia wondered to herself whether RJ would say it was time to wrap up and avoid revealing any more of her doubts and fears.

"Tell him I'm in an important meeting and will be a little longer, Maria," said RJ. "Maybe he can grab a sandwich next door. He knows that menu by heart." She winked at Sophia.

The office door closed. Sophia waited for RJ to continue, wondering if she would disclose more. With a pained look in her eyes, RJ asked, "So what do you think, Sophia? Have you worked with a team like mine before?"

She noticed that RJ skillfully moved the conversation from herself back to the team. "I wonder if RJ is willing to do the deep reflection and truth-telling—to work on herself first rather than insist it is the team that needs the support?" Sophia asked herself.

Sophia was all too familiar with leaders who thought everyone else was to blame for what ailed the company. At the first sign of a challenge, they canceled programs that built positive relationships and eliminated their coaching budgets. Sophia could feel her gut tighten as she remembered the president's betrayal that prompted her forced resignation.

"Yes, RJ. I have worked with teams that have similar challenges as the ones you describe. In those situations, however, I recommended that the leader of the team begin professional coaching first, to guide and sustain their own journey of self-reflection so they could decide who they wanted to be as a leader. A coaching engagement can support you in uncovering what you want most for yourself . . . as a human being and as a leader," Sophia said.

Sophia continued. "I suggest we start with a few introductory coaching sessions to get to know one another and address the concerns you just shared about having the full weight of the company on your shoulders and any other things that arise in confidential coaching conversations. At the end of those introductory sessions, we will know whether I am the best coach for you and whether you are willing to become accountable for being the person and leader you say you want to be. How does that sound?"

RJ sat back in the large chair and said, "You want to start with just me, without my team? I want the team to work better and get better results for the company, so it seems like they should be the focus."

"Yes, I agree and that is the desired outcome eventually. As you stated a moment ago, it starts with you and who you are being as a leader and human being. Taking the time for yourself to explore your self-doubts and get some relief from the weight of the company being solely on your shoulders, while trusting and inspiring others to bring their creativity to work. I am hearing that is what you want. Is that correct?" asked Sophia.

"Yes. That's it exactly," RJ confirmed, looking astonished. It was as if, until that moment, RJ had never said out loud what she wanted, much less heard someone mirror it back to her.

"It's a good start," said Sophia, "to know what you want, even if it feels vague at first." RJ was listening intently now. She leaned forward and rested her chin in the palm of her right hand.

RJ then sat back in the large chair and restated with an incredulous tone, "So you want to start with coaching just me? I don't really have a lot of time right now. Maria has me booked back to back every day. "But"—she paused. "Let's try a few conversations and see what happens. I can call Maria in now so we can find a time for tomorrow," she declared.

"You do take charge, RJ!" Sophia said with a grin. "I'm taking a day of personal time off tomorrow; something I scheduled a while back," said Sophia. "But we'll find a time that works soon."

RJ looked astonished. "You work for yourself and *you* schedule your own PTO? That's amazing. I almost never take time off . . . and I'm the CEO!" she exclaimed.

Sophia saw that self-care was likely to figure into their coaching conversations. She wondered whether RJ had ever experienced any truly rejuvenating self-care practice, aside from what she guessed were infrequent vacations.

"I'll email you a simple contract that covers confidentiality, my fees, and other important details to get us started," she said. "Let's schedule time now while I'm here." She and RJ and Maria quickly found times for the first few appointments over the next several weeks.

As Sophia stood to leave, RJ opened the door for her. "Well, Sophia, let's see where this goes."

Sophia smiled. "Yes, let's trust the process and see where it leads," she said, and headed to her car.

# 3

## What Brings You Joy?

Sophia drove home reflecting on her meeting with RJ. Overall, she was pleased with her approach during their coaching session. She hadn't been overeager and had remained curious, quieting her own internal chatter to look like a competent and professional coach. She had also listened for signs that RJ was willing to do her own personal work rather than insist it was her team that needed help. It wasn't clear yet if RJ would take responsibility for her own contribution to the company's poor engagement scores. For that reason, Sophia felt pleased about her instinct to suggest a short-term introductory coaching contract. A brief engagement would allow the two of them to get to know each other and hopefully for RJ to experiment with some new ways of listening and relating to herself and her team.

She was reminded of why she loved living in the Northwest. It was one of those sparkling spring days, warmth and sunlight filling the air. She pulled into the driveway and noticed her potted begonias had just begun to bloom. Bordering the front porch was a rainbow of flowerpots, each of which Sophia planted with a trio of flowering plants that now sported tender buds. Before long the pots would be topped by clouds of red, orange, and golden-yellow blossoms.

Sophia parked in her garage and headed into the house. She quickly deposited her bags on the kitchen counter, eager to go out to the porch to check on her pots. She filled the big watering can to the brim and took her time with each plant, hovering over the new begonias, coaxing them out.

As a little girl whose mother loved gardening, Sophia learned the importance of removing the dead flowers to make room for beautiful new blooms. "That's what life keeps calling us to do, too," she thought. "Remove the old to cultivate the new." She smiled as she emptied the watering can.

Bright sunlight always made the kitchen feel cozy and beautiful. Sophia fixed her favorite lunch: a green salad with a side of hummus, sliced turkey, and a tall glass of chilled tea.

Sophia finished lunch and placed her dishes in the sink when she heard a familiar ring from her tablet and knew it was Tara calling. As she reached to answer it, Sophia wondered what her life would have been like if she had never met her good friend Tara.

\* \* \*

Over fifteen years ago, not long after the breakup of her marriage, Sophia drove to the beach for a much-needed week of rest and recuperation. She rented a small cottage about half a mile from the beach trailhead. On her second evening there, Sophia struck out on the trail, which quickly turned onto a series of rustic cedar-beam stairs. As she hiked down through ferns and tall evergreens, Sophia soon found herself on a wide, quiet stretch of beach. For some time, she followed along the base of a high bluff, lost in thought. Then she sensed someone and looked up.

Against the sunset stood a woman peering into a grove of knee-high thick grass. She looked pensive, focused on the wet clumps, and held a pair of clippers in one hand and a large basket in the other. Sophia paused for a moment and simply watched. "What is she doing?" Sophia wondered. "I think she is looking for something in the grass."

The woman's stature communicated a strength and comfortableness with the land. She had on a well-worn jacket and muddy boots, and her long black hair was loosely tied back. Her silhouette was painted by the backdrop of the sunset with strands of light in vivid orange, gold, and pink dipping against the dark purple Olympic mountain range.

Sophia turned to walk back in the direction of her cabin so as not to bother the woman, when out of the corner of her eye Sophia noticed the woman was motioning to her—a gentle wave that signaled, "This way, over here." Sophia was puzzled and wondered to herself, "Is she motioning to me?" Sophia looked around and saw no one else and decided to wave back to the woman.

The woman waved again, but this time she had a bright blue scarf in her hand, gently lifting it into the spring breeze, meant to get Sophia's attention. Sophia now understood. She recognized her scarf that just a few minutes prior was wrapped around her own shoulders and under the hood of her jacket. Sophia smiled and walked briskly toward the woman, waving back, and nodding to signal, "Yes, it's mine! I must have dropped it."

"Thank you," Sophia said, with a slight bow of her head. "You are very kind to pick up my scarf and get my attention." Sophia smiled gratefully and took the scarf from the woman's hand, noticing how eloquent lines of age and wisdom beautifully sculptured her face.

"You are welcome. I am pleased it caught in this grass and I could retrieve it," the woman said.

Sophia leaned slightly forward and peeked into the woman's basket and saw the neatly arranged wet grass. The woman's kind spirit and the warmth of her presence made Sophia feel immediately at ease. Sophia was curious about the grass and beautiful basket but chose not to invade her privacy with questions.

"The spring is the best time to harvest the grass for the baskets I make. Once dried and properly prepared the grass becomes strong and pliable," the woman said, sensing Sophia's desire to learn more. With a gentle nod of her head, the woman said, "Hello, my name is Tara."

Happy to engage more, Sophia said, "Thank you again for my scarf. My name is Sophia, and I am staying at a local cabin this week. I so enjoy walking on this lovely beach, especially at sunset." They talked for a few minutes more, and at last Sophia got the courage to ask whether Tara would return to the beach the next day, hoping for a chance to talk again.

"Yes," said Tara, "I will be here tomorrow evening to harvest more grass from this grove."

Sophia took a risk. "Would it be okay if I walk here tomorrow night and say hello again?"

"Of course," Tara replied.

Sophia smiled and thanked Tara again for her scarf, then turned to walk back toward her cabin. After a few steps she looked over her shoulder to watch the captivating woman again. Sophia saw Tara walking away from the grove, slowly and rhythmically with each step, as though wading through the sand, each step rolling into the next.

It was so easy to talk with Tara those first few evenings. Sophia learned about Tara's Indigenous heritage and her role as director of the local tribal museum—her kind and peaceful heart, and her family that had lived in the area for generations. The words flowed out of Sophia as she found herself saying things that she had told no one else. Tara listened quietly as Sophia spoke about how difficult the last few years had been as, day by day, she had woken up to the increasing troubles in her marriage.

The beach cottage where Sophia stayed for that first week became a favorite retreat, one she always longed to revisit. One night she wrote in her journal simply, *This place nurtures and replenishes my soul. It feels like a true home.*

Sophia's evening walks on the beach with Tara were wonderful, but the location had become special to her for another reason. It was later that first week that Tara introduced Sophia to her funny, wise friend Ted, who came there often now that he was semiretired. By the end of the first week, Sophia returned home refreshed, rejuvenated, and with two new friends who quite literally changed the direction of her life.

\* \* \*

Sophia reached for her iPad and clicked the video button. There was Tara's smiling face. "Shh." Tara pointed, placing her finger to her lips. "I have a new hummingbird feeder and it's already attracting these beautiful ones. Look." Gently Tara picked up her iPad. She walked to a window and pointed the camera toward the feeder that hung just outside. Sophia watched the hummingbird as it hovered, taking in the sugary syrup.

"It gives me such joy to see them," Tara said. "Did you know they can flap their wings fifty times a second and fly forward or backward in the blink of an eye?" Tara turned and walked quietly back to the living room chair where she usually sat during their video calls.

With a relaxing sigh Tara said, "Ahh, the hummingbird. So much joy." She continued, "So, Sophia. How are you doing? What brings you joy today?"

"That's a beautiful question, Tara. I was just on the front porch watering the flowers. It gives me joy to nurture my flowers and watch their spring blooms emerge."

"Yes," agreed Tara. "It is a joy to take care of nature and to know that our attention and protection can create an environment where all can thrive. I believe we are created to help support nature and to live in harmony with the earth, so when we act on that purpose, it is natural to feel joy."

Tara paused and suddenly Sophia's screen went dark. Tara returned almost as quickly. "Sorry," she said. "This technology is still a mystery to me. I accidentally touched the wrong button, I guess. But now I've brought you back!" She grinned.

Sophia laughed. "It's great to connect so easily, even with a few glitches now and then. It's a privilege to appreciate the hummingbirds with you today. More and more I realize how nurtured I feel when I allow myself to fully experience and honor nature. Whether it is walking in the neighborhood park, working the soil in my yard, or listening to the songbirds as I wake—it is all balm for my soul in these stressful times," Sophia said.

Sophia paused and looked into the screen. "Tara, how are you today?"

"I am well, overall. Thank you for asking," Tara said. "As you know, my brother, Paco, has been seriously ill for a while. He's doing well now, and I admit my spirits are lifted when he's in remission. He's been my best friend since we were kids. Our quality time together, laughing, reminiscing, and deeply connecting is what nurtures my spirit right now."

Sophia nodded and affirmed Tara's appreciation for her brother. She waited to see if Tara wanted to say more. When she did not, Sophia reflected on her day. "I saw a new client this morning, and at the end of our session she told me that she rarely takes a day off work. It got me thinking about why it is so important to have a self-care practice. As you know, Tara, I have struggled over the years with taking care of myself, thinking that if I loved my work, then self-care, relaxing, and rejuvenation is unnecessary.

"I have such a strong need to be of service and make a difference in the world, so it is easy for me to overwork and constantly strive to do more. Sometimes I confuse my desire to be of service with the realization that overworking serves no one, especially not me!

*41* △

"You have helped me to understand, Tara, the need to make room for joy and to nurture my spirit so I can be my best self and contribute to a better world. I never want to miss my trips to the beach to see you and take time to relax, but still . . . sometimes . . . I have conflicting thoughts. I assume that if I focus on my own needs, I am selfish and shirking my duty to be of service to others. Intellectually I know that can't be true, but the thought is still there."

Tara smiled. "That's a powerful insight, Sophia."

"Thanks, Tara. There are so many complex and scary things happening in the world," Sophia continued. "I can get fatigued trying to figure out which problem to tackle and just how I can best serve. I coach my clients to include self-care in their lives and then I wonder if I should include it in my own!" she admitted to Tara.

"Everything you say is true, Sophia. In our busy culture self-care often means getting a massage, spending a day with friends, getting a manicure, or going out for drinks, sometimes drinking too much. We fool ourselves thinking that is self-care that will sustain us. Those episodes may refresh us somewhat, but I definitely don't think that's the kind of self-care that each human being requires."

Sophia nodded. "I have discovered, through our conversations and your mentoring, that what matters most is my intention. My intention supports whatever self-care I choose. It doesn't have to be a long vacation or massages, which are nice, but now I have learned that taking time to care for my flowers, to offer them food, water, and care is a privilege, not an obligation. I can replenish my soul moment to moment if that is my intention." She paused.

Tara said, "That's beautiful, Sophia. I think of self-care as the way Mother spirit cares for us all. A mature mother meets her own needs first, so that she has the capability to care for her child. When she doesn't meet her own needs, she is depleted and will eventually feel resentful. But you probably know that already, don't you?" Tara added with a pleasant smile.

Sophia nodded in agreement, enthusiastically adding, "When I don't take responsibility for meeting my own needs, I end up looking to others or things outside me to fill me up, hoping someone, some job, or some other 'thing' will sustain me. I certainly did that when the president invited me to create a company-wide coaching program. I got so attached to that project that I was sure it was the fulfilling work I craved. I have fallen into that trap more times than I want to count!" Sophia sheepishly admitted.

"No one else can fill our heart with meaning and fulfillment. We try looking all around, everywhere but in here." Tara touched her heart. "That's when we miss the love and wisdom already speaking in our heart. Such a person lives in a state of craving that is never satisfied. Their inner wisdom is covered up with too much doing and having, always running here and there. Such a person cannot see beyond themselves. They often say things like, 'Nobody understands what I'm going through. No one is supporting me.' Such thinking leads to a Victim mentality."

"What you just described, Tara, is one of the fastest ways I get trapped in the Dreaded Drama Triangle. I know I can slip into the Victim role, feeling persecuted by all the people or things 'out there' that didn't satisfy me. If I don't get what I think I need from them to fill the hole inside of me, I start blaming others or the circumstances, judging them as the problem and the cause of my suffering. Once I do that, I start looking for a Rescuer to soothe my uncomfortable feelings. Often the relief I seek for my pain is overworking, staying busy, an extra glass of wine, or other ways to distract myself—none of which is self-care!"

Tara glanced upward and away from the screen for a moment, appearing to have a new insight, then asked Sophia, "May I share something my mother impressed upon me when I was a little girl?"

"Of course, Tara. Please," Sophia urged.

"My mother would often say that we must 'empty our vessels.' As a young girl I had no idea what she was talking about, but gradually as I grew older I began to understand the wisdom behind the image of emptying my vessel. This modern world is filled with demands and limitless to-do lists—we're endlessly working and striving for success, as you often say. Many people spend their lives, bodies, and minds, working so hard to build an identity they hope will make them feel successful. But that way leads us far away from ourselves and our community. How can it be success to live so disconnected?

"If we constantly strive to meet the demands of this culture of taking and getting, we only fill our vessel with more demands that can never be fulfilled. Doing this, we become lost, walking farther and farther away from a life of balance."

Sophia leaned closer to Tara's face on the screen.

Tara continued, "What I have learned, what I think my mother meant, is when you empty your vessel, you too will hear your own wisdom. You will know what you need to do or be, and you will accept yourself as you are. It's a journey we are all on, to balance our care for the world while first caring for ourselves."

With a gleam in her eye and a wry smile, Tara said, "Your vessel is strengthened by the way you care for it. How do you take care of anything that you value? How would you care for your vessel if it were your favorite thing? We must all discern how to care for ourselves, just as you care for your flowers. The way you care for your son.

"You would not deny the flowers water, would you? Of course not. We marvel at how tenderly they turn their blooms toward the sun, receiving nutrients that only the sun can provide. Like those flowers, we are each beautiful. We are sacred. Giving ourselves love and reverence is respecting the Great Spirit inside us all." Tara sighed.

"You are so wise!" Sophia said. "I love talking with you and our philosophical conversations."

"As I enjoy talking with you." Tara laughed.

Sophia jumped in. "What you are saying is so much more than the basic notion of self-care as I've typically thought of it. I mean, how can I be of service to the world unless I take care of myself? It isn't selfish at all. It is my first responsibility!" she said, feeling this new epiphany.

Tara added, "I think that is why my mother often said that self-care is world care. And I now realize that for anyone who wishes to bring about cultural change, self-care isn't just a responsibility—it's a revolutionary act. It is essential for all of us, of course, but especially for leaders, activists, coaches like yourself—for anybody who seeks to transform oppression, trauma, and injustice. This is how we will fill our vessel with wisdom, the best nourishment of all, for you and everyone you know."

"We definitely need change," agreed Sophia. "Modern culture is a pressure cooker: working hard, pressure to produce more and better results. I often hear my clients say they believe that taking time off work, especially time for self-care, is wasted time. Like my client this morning, who said she almost never takes time for herself. I feel sad seeing how, in our culture, we get stuck in that ruthless pattern.

"I am still learning self-care for myself. Our calls are self-care for me, for sure. And, my long weekend at the beach is coming up in a few weeks, too, and I'm not going to let anything interfere with the chance to see you," Sophia said, adding, "and to take care of myself."

"Let's talk again soon. You can call me anytime, Sophia. I enjoy our friendship, too. I am signing off now and going to enjoy the hummingbirds again." Tara smiled broadly and waved goodbye before the screen went dark.

Sophia sat motionless for a few moments after Tara left the call. She consciously took several long, deep breaths. With those slow breaths she felt the wisdom of caring for herself, of loving the mystery of her body and how it replenished her if she gave it rest, nourishing food and water, and if she extended an open and kind heart and authentically connected with those she loved. Her body and spirit instinctively knew how to care for themselves if she was willing to listen.

# 4

# I Don't Know *How* to Relax!

As Sophia waited with her cup of tea on her desk near the monitor, RJ's face popped up on the screen of her tablet. "Hello, RJ, nice to see you!" she said, beaming.

"Hi," said RJ, appearing distracted, straightening a few items on her desk. "Nice to see you, too."

To kick off the session, Sophia asked, "I'm curious, what's going well for you today?"

RJ frowned slightly. Leaning back, she said, "Well *that's* an interesting question I don't get asked every day! Let me think about that.

"We sold three new homes in the last week. That's huge for us, given the economic challenges right now, so that has gone well. I can't think of anything, really, that has gone well just today, though."

Clearly on her guard, RJ asked, "So, how's this coaching thing supposed to work?"

"Well," Sophia began, "we touched on a few things during our first meeting last week—the outcomes you said you wanted. Let's start there and see what else surfaces that you may want to focus on during our coaching time. Do you remember the outcomes we summarized together, the things you said you wanted from coaching?"

RJ looked up and away, then back to the screen. "I remember you saying you were taking personal time off. And I said that I wouldn't know what to do if I took a day off. Oh, and you asked me what bothers me most, and I remember saying I feel like the weight of the whole company is on my shoulders. And that I get really tired sometimes. So those are the main things, I guess, that have stayed with me. I'm not sure what the outcomes were, if we talked about those," RJ said.

Sophia too remembered their conversation about taking time off, especially after her conversation with Tara about self-care and why it is so essential in today's often stressful world. Sophia also remembered that RJ said she wanted to inspire her team but that instead she often criticized their ideas and was quick to say why they wouldn't work. Sophia decided to leave the 'time off' topic for now and ask a follow-up question about RJ's team.

"How are things going with your team?"

"No different, really." RJ said. "I have a long list of complaints about my team, but I try not to talk about them all the time."

Sophia began, "RJ, a complaint can be good sometimes because it points out what you *don't* want. You can learn, however, to see a complaint as a door that leads you toward what you *do* want. That is a useful way to understand your complaints. Unless of course, you get *stuck* in complaining and never stop to ask what you really want. I often say that behind every complaint is a commitment.*

RJ looked puzzled. "Could you say that last thing again, a little slower this time?"

"Do you mean the point that behind every complaint there's a commitment? That may seem like an odd statement, but if you think about it, we don't complain about things we don't care about, do we? So, rather than feel victimized by and powerless to change what you don't want—your complaint—the secret is to examine your complaint and get really curious about it, to discover the commitment behind it.

"But if you go on automatic pilot and continue to complain, if you resist getting curious about what's behind your complaint, you can get stuck and become a Victim to your own complaining."

"That's exactly how I feel," RJ said. "Since you asked me about what bothers me, I have noticed all week that a lot of stuff bothers me, and I complain a lot. At least I think about the complaints I have, even though I may not say them out loud. You used the word *Victim*. I hate that word. When my dad died and I took over the company, I could see that some people, even our employees, felt sorry for me. The last thing I wanted was for people to see me as a Victim. It was my responsibility to take charge, and I told myself I'd never allow myself to act like a Victim."

RJ went on forcefully. "But now, maybe always having to 'buck up and soldier on' is having the opposite effect. Some days I feel like a Victim all day long!" She looked away again.

"My friend Roger from the Rotary, who referred me to you, said you showed him a drawing of a 'drama triangle.' He said it made sense to him and helped him a lot."

"I believe he was referring to what I call the Dreaded Drama Triangle or 'DDT' for short. When you get caught in the grip of the DDT, it has a toxic effect on your relationships with others and with yourself. I look forward to sharing it with you. Before I do, though, I want to share a concept that the DDT is founded upon. Okay to go there first?"

"Sure," said RJ.

Sophia continued, "During our coaching sessions I will use the phrase *human operating system*. Just as our smartphones and computers have operating systems, we human beings have one, too. Our human operating system has three basic parts. First, we think—we're cognitive beings. Second, we have an inner state, our emotions, that arises from our thoughts."

Sophia paused, smiling. "Are you with me so far?"

"I think so. Sort of," RJ said. "Go on."

"The third part of our operating system is that we take action," Sophia said. "This is the 'doing' part of life, our behavior. We do things."

"I get that one, for sure," said RJ. "Seems like I'm in constant motion all day, doing things."

"Right. That's pretty much the story of those of us living in the modern world. We're really good at keeping busy and getting things done, and not so good at understanding our emotions and the thoughts that motivate our actions.

"RJ, as you listen to the description of your human operating system, what's your thought about why we're starting with this idea?"

"Well . . . your description of an operating system makes sense to me. Every time our technology department wants money for a system upgrade, they tell me our current operating system is outdated and limits what we can do with our information systems. Another example I can think of is that we're upgrading our company trucks from gasoline to electric—which has an entirely different operating system—and that means our maintenance department needs new skills."

RJ picked up her phone and held it in front of the screen. "My darn phone is constantly giving me alerts that I need to update things, too, sometimes even when I wish it wouldn't, with new apps and options I didn't have before. And then it seems to take me about a week just to figure out what's changed. So I know an operating system matters."

"Exactly," said Sophia. "Those are all great examples that show why it's essential to understand our human operating system, in real time, while it is operating. If you aren't privy to the way you operate in the moment, your system will keep running the old and often outdated programs."

RJ looked away for a moment. "Okay," she said. "That makes sense. If I don't understand my own human operating system, I can't make upgrades. If my technology director doesn't understand our current operating system, he's not very resourceful. And if our mechanics don't know how to fix electric engines, our new trucks will be useless. And I need to be able to observe how my human operating system works in real time—is that the idea?"

"Yes, that's it exactly," said Sophia. "I use the acronym FISBE to describe our human operating

*This concept was developed by Harvard educators and psychologists Robert Kegan and Lisa Lahey.

system. The *F* stands for focus, your thoughts. *IS* stands for inner state, or your emotions, and *BE* stands for behavior, the actions you take. That's FISBE. It rhymes with Frisbee."

"Good," said RJ, smiling. "That'll help me remember it."

*Diagram 1. FISBE (Focus, Inner State, Behavior)*

"So let's apply the FISBE to your recognition that you complain a lot. Take a moment and think of a complaint. When you're ready, give me an example of something you complain about."

"There are so many," RJ said, rolling her eyes. "Okay, one of my complaints is about my director of construction, John. The last few months he's often been late for our Monday morning staff meeting. We've had Monday morning staff meetings for a long time, so he really should know by now that it's important. I've talked to him about it, and I've even yelled at him a couple of times, but he just never seems to get here on time. Being on time isn't too much to expect, is it?"

"Good example," said Sophia. "Okay, think back to the last time that happened. Take a few moments to relive the situation in your mind . . . got it?"

"Yes," said RJ. "That's easy. It happened again just yesterday morning!"

"All right, now let's apply the FISBE. When this happens, what is your focus? In other words, what are you thinking about?"

"I just get so angry, frustrated," said RJ.

"I understand your frustration. I can see it on your face now. That is the *IS*—the inner state, the emotional part of the human operating system that arises from your thoughts. What do you *think* about when John is late?"

RJ paused, frowning. "Just a moment. I need to think about that.

"I guess I'm thinking that John is not reliable. That if he is late with me, the boss, then he's probably late for everything else, and what a waste of time! I'm thinking he doesn't respect me. I'm thinking that if he has a poor work habit such as habitual lateness, then neither I nor my company are getting our money's worth and I should consider letting him go." RJ's face flushed red.

"Let me see if I understand what you're saying," said Sophia. "It sounds like you think that John is unreliable, and he may be a liability to you and your company, causing you to feel frustration and anger. Is that correct so far?"

"Yes, that's it," RJ shot back. "In fact, I'm boiling just thinking about it. Now you can understand why I complain about him so often."

"Okay," said Sophia. "Nice insights, RJ. Let's go now to the third part of the FISBE—the *BE*. What behaviors do you engage in? In this case what do you actually *do* when John is late? In other words, RJ, how do you behave?"

"Well, when he walks into the meeting, *late again*, I point out, sometimes sarcastically, that the rest of us all arrived on time. Sometimes I say something in front of everyone, thinking that maybe some degree of embarrassment will motivate him to get here promptly next time. After he comes in late, I'm basically fuming. So, I may cut people off sometimes or not even hear what people are saying because I'm so mad at him. I feel so disrespected!"

"I appreciate your honesty in sharing that, RJ," said Sophia. "How are you feeling now, after retelling that story?"

"I'm reliving the whole thing all over again. And I really don't understand why it upsets me so much."

"Got it," Sophia said. "That shows how powerful our thoughts are. Just thinking about it evokes strong emotions right now, even though it is just a thought. That is why it is essential to understand that your human operating system is linked to your thoughts. And here's the really important part. We tell ourselves we are just solving the problem—in this case the problem of John being late—but in reality, we are actually reacting to the anxious emotions the thought evokes."

"You bet I am reacting to it. I get really mad at John for not listening to me," RJ said. "But let's go on, because I could talk all day about the whole situation."

"Okay, let's do keep moving and apply the FISBE model to pull back the curtain on what's going on for you when John is late."

"Do we have to?" RJ said with a smirk. Then she waved it away. "I'm just kidding. Keep going."

Sophia smiled and continued. "Applying the FISBE model is like having a blueprint to help identify your focus in any situation. In this case, let's slow down now. Please take your time to reflect for a moment on your thoughts about John being late. What attitudes do you have about being on time?"

"Wow," said RJ. "When you asked that, right away I remembered how my dad was a real stickler about being on time. He demanded punctuality of everyone, didn't matter who it was. He got really mad if my sister, my mom, and I, and especially his workers, weren't on time. My stomach gets tied in knots even thinking about it." She paused.

"But that's not all. I believe being on time has helped me become a productive, successful CEO of this company. What would happen if *I* were irresponsible and didn't show up on time for leadership meetings and client appointments?"

"Thanks for that, RJ. I can see that this complaint about your director of construction being late has opened the door for a lot of emotions and memories. We also might say it has revealed the story you have about being on time. Does it make sense to you that I called it a story?"

RJ, visibly irritated, said, "But being on time has helped me get where I am, so I think it's a good value to have. If that is my story, then I plan to keep it."

"Now, there's a coaching question that is bubbling up for me. You hired me to ask questions, right?" Sophia said.

"I guess so," said RJ.

Sophia continued, "I am curious about what else might be going on in this situation. I'm wondering, are you unconsciously focusing on something else? Before you answer, take a couple of deep breaths and just sit with that question for a few moments."

RJ took a few breaths. Sophia could see that RJ's shoulders seemed to relax a little. "Hmm. What *else* am I focusing on," she murmured just loud enough for Sophia to hear.

"I'm a little embarrassed to say this, but I think I'm focusing on . . . that I'll look bad if I don't run a productive meeting. That my team won't respect me. I can hear Dad whispering in my ear, saying I'd better not let people run over me. So I guess that's what I am mostly focusing on."

Sophia could feel the energy in the moment, wondering what it felt like for RJ to become more aware of her long-buried thoughts about her father's judgment. "I love to dig deep," thought Sophia to herself, "but this is RJ's moment. It's not about me fulfilling my hope that she'll have a powerful insight."

"Thank you for your vulnerability, RJ," said Sophia. "My hunch is those thoughts have probably been there for a long time, running your human operating system."

RJ looked directly into the screen with a slight frown and showed no sign of wanting to speak.

Sophia continued. "This is an example of how the FISBE can help you look at the relationship between your thoughts, feelings, and behavior. So, I have a little homework for you to consider between now and next week when we meet again. You may not have realized when you signed up for coaching that you would have homework, did you?" Sophia smiled.

"I'd like for you to play with this idea: What other thoughts might you consider regarding John being late? What are some other thoughts that could be true about that situation?" Sophia then asked, "Are you open to giving it a try?"

"I'm not sure I know what you mean. Can you give me an example?"

"Here's one thought, and it is just an example, so it may not 'land' for you," said Sophia. "One thought might be, 'John is late because he is very friendly and says hello to everyone on his way to your office' or 'John is a good construction manager and being late is actually a minor problem as long as he is good at his job.' Those are just two examples of different thoughts about John being late."

"I sort of see what you mean now. I can try. But I've been having those same thoughts about John being late for so long that I may not be able to come up with any new ones."

"That's all right," said Sophia. "You don't actually have to have entertained those new thoughts or believe them. *Just consider* having a different thought at this point. Are you committed to that baby step, RJ?"

"Yes. I can do that."

"Great. We can start there next time. Before we wrap up this session, I want to hear more about the other thing you said had stayed with you since we talked—that you don't take personal time off. Let's apply the FISBE model to look at that issue for a few minutes. Okay?"

"Okay," RJ said, taking a deep breath. She looked at her watch and arched her shoulders toward her neck. Her body language signaled she might not be comfortable with this subject.

Sophia continued. "Regarding the situation of not taking personal time off, what is your focus? What do you think about?"

"That's pretty easy. There's too much to do, and no one else can do what I do. If I take time off, the company will go downhill." RJ paused and looked down for what seemed like a full minute.

"You know, now that I hear myself say that, I hear another voice, too. Didn't know there were so many voices in my head all talking at the same time!" she said.

"That other voice says, 'You will be seen as really lazy if you just take time off whenever you feel like it.'"

"Bet I can guess whose voice that was!" said Sophia. But before she could say more, RJ blurted out, "My dad!" They both chuckled and RJ smiled bigger than Sophia had seen her smile before.

RJ went on. "Actually, I have been noticing how I let Dad run my life . . . and he's not even *here*. I don't seem to focus on what I really want. Even saying that makes me cringe because, of course, I'm an independent person. I'm smart and strong-willed. Always have been. I run a multimillion-dollar company that has been profitable every year but two in the last twenty-five, and those were during the Great Recession when the housing market completely stalled. RJ Construction provides jobs for over five hundred people. I'm really proud of all that, so it's kind of a shock to say I don't have a sense of who I am or how to take personal time off. No wonder I feel so tired." RJ sighed.

"I had always assumed I would follow in his footsteps. Mom made it clear ever since I can remember that she didn't want anything to do with running this business, so I was gradually trained by my dad to take over. My younger sister was never interested in the business, either, so it was understood that I'd be the one to lead the company someday. It was a done deal from the time I was a teenager. I even got my college degree in construction management. I just didn't know, of course, that Dad would die so young, that he wouldn't be here to show me the ropes of the day-to-day. I have some hard-earned skills and successes and I'm proud of those. But I still have this gnawing feeling something isn't right.

"Sophia," RJ went on, "the truth is, I don't know *how* to relax. How could I take a vacation without being constantly in touch with the office? I've been told that some people here *wish* I would take time off. My sister tells me all the time I'm a workaholic, but I can't help it. I've never known anything else really. What the heck would I *do* on a vacation? Or even on a day off? Unless I were sick or something."

Sophia saw the depth of RJ's sadness, as well as how skilled she had become at avoiding her feelings. How hard it must be to not even be able to *imagine* a day to just relax! Sophia eagerly looked forward to her beach retreats, to the long walks talking and joking with her friends Tara and Ted. She turned her attention back to what RJ was sharing.

"It's a totally foreign concept, I'm afraid," said RJ. "I'm proud of the company's many successes, but I'm beginning to wonder, what is all this *for*? I've achieved pretty much everything I set out to do—build this business and prove to myself and everyone else that I could do it. But now what? I don't have time for a relationship, or even for family, really. Except now and then going to watch my nephew's and my niece's soccer games."

Sophia remained silent for a moment and observed RJ sitting with her reflection.

"You've uncovered a lot about your thinking and how it has run your life so far," said Sophia. "I appreciate how open you've been today." She paused to see if RJ wanted to say more. RJ looked pensive. After a few moments of silence, Sophia continued.

"Our time is almost up for now. We talked about homework to consider other possible thoughts around John's being late. I also encourage you to give yourself a break. Go a little easy on yourself," Sophia said, looking directly into the computer screen and meeting RJ's eyes. "If you can't go easy on yourself yet, then consider the possibility that *maybe* you could someday go easy," Sophia said with a smile, knowing it would be a challenge for her.

"Okay, Sophia. I'll try. Thank you," said RJ. "This is quite a process," she added.

"Yes, it is," said Sophia. "All right, see you next week. I'll send you a video link. Take care."

# 5

## Tell Three Stories

Sophia wondered what this second video call with RJ would hold. So much had come to light in their first session. Sophia took a deep breath and prepared for the session with her usual ritual. She placed a candle on the mantel next to a small vase of bright yellow flowers. As she lit the candle, she set her intention to be open and curious. Then she sat down with a cup of tea, opened her laptop, and clicked the link.

Soon her client's face appeared. "Hello, RJ. Nice to see you again."

"It's nice to see you, too," RJ said, adjusting her screen so the light from a lamp on her desk was not in her eyes.

"There, that's better. I can see you better now without that glare. I'd like to jump right in," said Sophia.

"Fine with me. My day is booked to the max," RJ responded.

"I'm curious, RJ. Has anything become clearer for you since our last session?"

RJ looked puzzled. "I'm not sure . . . I got really stuck doing your homework about John and coming up with different thoughts about why he is late. I'm beginning to see that if I have an opinion about someone or something, I totally believe it as a fact. The homework was *hard*."

"Thanks for your honesty. It's amazing, isn't it, how quickly and easily our minds stick to one judgment and opinion? Our egos seem to think we can be unique individuals only if we cling to our opinions. I learned the hard way that my judgments become like the details in a plot—a story I make up to explain whatever is happening. And then my brain keeps looking for details to embellish that story. Why do you think our brains do that, RJ? I mean, what is it about human nature that is so ready to make a snap judgment and stick to it, sometimes even after new information is revealed that contradicts our story?"

"I guess because people like being right, don't we? I know I do," RJ proclaimed.

"I think that is basically it. There is a certain comfortableness about being right. If I don't understand something, or I feel threatened, like all other humans I'm quick to make up my own details to fill in the blanks."

"That makes sense," said RJ. "As I was considering different thoughts about John and why he's always late, it felt like my brain wouldn't allow me to think a new thought. I was really stuck in the one and only thought that I know was *right*!" RJ's smirk let on that now she wasn't so sure.

Sophia nodded. "Once we have that story in place, we project from the past to the future and back to the present, searching out, or even inventing, details that seem to confirm our theory as a fact. That's how we end up reinforcing the same old opinions we've always held. It is actually an impressive strategy in the sense that it's so effective. But unfortunately, it can really limit your perspective. In the field of psychology, it's called *confirmation bias*. That bias makes it hard to see what's really true and what's only a story we told ourselves to feel more comfortable with an unfamiliar idea or a new situation. That's why it's so powerful when we ask the question we talked about last time: 'Where are you putting your focus?' It takes some time and reflection to see and sort through all the different layers of meaning we've created with our thinking. I once had a client who said that when she writes her memoir, the title will be *My Life as an Onion*."

They both laughed, and then RJ leaned in.

"So, about that homework you gave me. At first, I thought I knew what my focus was—John coming in late. But then I realized that wasn't *really* what I was focusing on. My real focus is worrying whether I will live up to Dad's example by running a tight ship here at the company. Part of that would mean people coming in on time. I did come up with a few new possible thoughts, as you suggested. But I'm not sure if they're what you had in mind."

"Great," said Sophia. "I'd like to hear them."

"Okay, here's one: 'John has an old rattletrap car that keeps breaking down and causing him to be late. But he doesn't mention it, because he doesn't want us to know he drives such an old car.'"

"Nice one. That sounds plausible. Any others?"

"Yes. 'John is very independent and being late is his way of maintaining independence from his strong-willed boss: me.' And here's one more: 'John is such a creative builder and designer that he gets lost in his early morning artistic moments and loses track of time.'"

"Great job, RJ. Three very different possible thoughts about what may be going on with John. What was valuable for you about that homework?"

RJ stared at Sophia with a puzzled look, her eyes tense, as though searching her brain for an answer.

"I guess realizing it's important to be able to generate different points of view," RJ said. "I know that intellectually, but it's hard to remember when my job is all about making quick judgments and decisions. I have to keep things moving."

"I get that, RJ. You do have a big challenge—to be a strong, decisive leader while at the same time remaining open-minded. If you become attached to only one point of view, you will close down without listening, hearing, and possibly benefiting from, other creative possibilities. Relying on your judgment alone means you will miss a lot of information. In complex business situations, such automatic judgments are too limiting to support you in being the kind of leader, the person, you say you want to be. One who listens, one whose employees and leadership team are willing to share ideas. And it's a worthy goal, because listening for alternatives makes for better business decisions. In personal relationships as well, when we cling to snap judgments and our familiar strong opinions, we automatically stop listening, which in turn fosters distrust and yields poor relationships."

"Hmm," said RJ. "Maybe that's why our company's trust scores were so low. Dad always told me the company tone starts at the top. He *definitely* had strong opinions, and that was one of them!" She chuckled. "But are you saying that others around here know I typically ignore their ideas because I've already made up my mind? Do you think maybe they don't trust me to listen to what's on *their* minds?"

"Your strongly voiced opinions could be giving others that impression, yes. I don't know enough about the culture there yet to say for sure."

Sophia continued, reflecting back what she had heard: "RJ, you seem to be noticing that you have a mental habit of sticking to judgmental thoughts. And it sounds as if now you're also wondering if that habit may be affecting how well your business runs. Does that sound right?"

"Maybe so," said RJ. "I want to be a strong leader like my dad was, but I definitely don't want to shut down good ideas."

"We often pick out what we pay attention to, choosing to hear only the bits of information that reinforce our favored ways of thinking, or that support our point in a discussion," Sophia offered. "We don't do this consciously—in most cases, it just happens automatically. But it's a pattern that keeps running in the background of our minds unless we become alert to it."

"This is feeling like a lot of work. To completely change the way I think . . . to retool my whole operating system!" RJ looked distressed.

"RJ, we all do this," Sophia said, hoping to encourage her. "So, it's essential to have a heap of compassion for our human operating system. If we become judgmental of ourselves, without compassion for our efforts, we just compound the challenge. We end up judging our judgments."

"Okay, I think I see what you mean," said RJ. "But you make it all sound so simple, and it's not. You are asking me to let down my guard a lot more, and I'm not sure that's such a good idea. I've taken this company to a new level of success by staying focused and being persuasive. And yes, strong-willed, too. It seems like all this listening and being open to others' ideas is going to take a lot of time and slow down the critical decisions that have to be made. I can just see the deadlines whizzing past!"

Sophia wondered whether RJ was going to stick to her original intention for coaching. Was she really serious about personal development? She reminded herself that RJ had originally wanted her to work with her team and was surprised when Sophia suggested she start working with her one on one. She reminded herself that people change on their own timetable, that each person must walk their own path. Sophia's job as a coach was to trust her client's process.

"RJ," Sophia continued, "I'd like to share a quick story about how I learned that creating new or different stories can open up the mind and heart and, ultimately, shift our focus toward what we want. Okay if I share a personal story?"

"Sure, let's hear it," said RJ, relaxing a bit as the focus shifted away from her.

"This happened several years ago when my son, Gabe, who was nine years old at the time, asked me to drive him to school. He wanted to get there early so he would have time to shoot hoops out on the playground with a few of his buddies. As we pulled out of the driveway, Gabe was tossing his basketball from hand to hand. It was easy to see he was excited.

"About a mile from the school we got stuck behind a very slow, dilapidated flatbed pickup with a large refrigerator tied down in the back. Two people, a man and a woman, were sitting in front. The truck was barely moving. Gabe started complaining, 'Aw, come on! Why can't they go faster?!' It was obvious he was going to miss his hoop time if that truck didn't move out of the way, and he was getting really exasperated.

"That's when I pulled out a timeless parenting trick—distraction. I started a game we had often played in the car before. I asked Gabe to get curious about why the driver might be going so slow. He thought for a moment and said, 'The truck is so old that it doesn't have enough power to go any faster.' Then he added, 'The man's afraid if he speeds up, that refrigerator's going to fall over.'

"'Those are good ones,' I told Gabe. Then I said I had a story, too: 'The woman in the front seat is nine months pregnant and the man is worried that if he goes faster and hits a bump, she will go into labor and have the baby right there in the truck!' Gabe laughed, and at that point, his imagination really took off. He said, 'I think aliens dropped that refrigerator in the back of the truck . . . and the driver is scared if he goes faster, the refrigerator will tip over and make the aliens mad!'

"By the time Gabe and I pulled up to the school grounds, we were still laughing about his alien story. I kissed him goodbye and told him to have fun." Sophia paused for effect.

"RJ, as I watched my son hop out of the car and run into school that morning, I had the essential experience of coaching—of not being attached to the problem. That truck was right in front of us, blocking our way, but instead of getting irritated along with my son, I paused just long enough to open my mind and heart to consider additional possibilities. And it made all the difference in our morning. That was a powerful lesson for me, personally and professionally. What we focus on creates our reality."

RJ grinned. "That's a great story."

"That experience inspired a coaching exercise that I use a lot now. It's called Tell Three Stories. That was the homework I asked you to do, and you did it quite well."

Sophia continued, "It's important to thoroughly examine our focus. Because our brains are constantly scanning the environment on high alert, looking for danger. And it's not always physical danger that makes us perk up. For example, Gabe's worry was about the social 'threat' of missing hoop time with his buddies and risking damage to his social connections. If we're unconscious as to how our nervous system takes over when it senses any kind of danger, physical or social, our mind will default to focusing on that perceived problem.

"Applying the FISBE helps you to explore your focus. You can begin to see the emotions that arise from your thinking, as well as the behavior you choose in response to that emotion. When my son was focused on the slow truck and the social threat of missing out on shooting hoops with his friends, he got agitated and started complaining. His brain was riveted to that threat."

RJ interjected, "And when he started to focus on being creative and came up with that cool alien story, his creative juices got flowing, so he felt better and started laughing—he relaxed. I think I'm seeing how our emotions change with our focus."

"Exactly!" said Sophia. "When you shift your thinking," she added, "your emotions shift, too."

Sophia continued, "Let's check in, RJ. How are you feeling right now? We have a few minutes left in our session here. Would you like to keep going?"

"I'm okay for now," said RJ, straightening in her chair. "Let's keep going."

"Let's build on these new insights about how we think. You could start by asking what you usually listen for. When I ask that question, 'What do you listen for?' what's the first thing that comes to mind?"

RJ suddenly pushed back, her neck and shoulders tight. "What do I listen for? Well, to be honest, I've never really thought about it." She paused a moment, then said, "I'm thinking now about some of the conversations I have with people here at the office. What I listen for . . . are the problems people are having, so I can give them advice about what to do to solve those problems."

"So you've gotten into the habit of listening for problems to solve. Would you say that's basically it?"

"Yes, I think that sums it up," said RJ.

"Okay," said Sophia. "There's a powerful framework for reflecting on the way to listen that I want to share. It is called the Three Levels of Listening. Guess I like things that come in threes, don't I? First the

Tell Three Stories exercise and now the Three Levels of Listening." She chuckled. "Here's a quick look at the Three Levels of Listening.

"The first level is called Listening to Be Right. At this level you listen for whether you disagree or agree with what someone is saying. You listen for information that affirms your point of view. And if your opinions differ from what the other person is saying, you listen for opportunities to jump into the conversation, share your opposing point of view, and win the point. Collaboration and working well together is very difficult when you're listening at this level. Basically, this level of listening is all about 'me' and 'Do I agree or disagree?'" Sophia asked RJ, "Does that sound familiar?"

"Yes, it does," said RJ with a wry smile. "And I can see why you're bringing it up. What's the second level?"

"The second level is called Listening for Possibilities," Sophia said. At this level you suspend your judgments and focus on what the other person is saying. Rather than jumping in to talk, you listen deeply to the other person and what they are sharing. You move your focus away from yourself and your own views, and onto them."

Sophia continued, "At this level of listening, you get curious and genuinely want to learn more. The questions you ask arise from the information the other person is sharing. Your focus is on what they want, more than on what they *don't* want, and you listen for the wide range of possibilities available to them."

"Okay, makes sense," said RJ. "I'm trying to imagine what the third level is. The second one is going to be hard enough. I have a feeling this is going to be my next homework assignment." She smiled.

"The choice is always yours," said Sophia. After a brief pause, she went on.

"I call the third level Listening for Collaboration. In this level, you listen from Level Two (Listening for Possibilities), plus you go even deeper to sense the energy or feeling tone embedded in what the other person is saying, or maybe in what they're not saying. At this third level, you listen with your intuition, and your attention goes to the creativity that wants to emerge. It is at this level that, with inspiration and excitement, new ideas and innovations are ignited."

"Sophia, I think you were listening to me at that second level, and maybe also at the third level, in our first session," said RJ. "I remember you saying that you sensed that I was focusing on something else. You must have been tapping into that deeper listening. It made a big impression when you asked me that. I wondered how you picked up on it."

"Being listened to in Level Two and Three is a wonderful thing," agreed Sophia. "We feel seen, heard, and loved. RJ, can you think of someone who has listened to you at Level Two, Listening for Possibilities, and at Level Three, Listening for Collaboration?"

RJ looked off into the distance. Sophia could see a sparkle in RJ's eyes as she began to smile, remembering. "Only one person, really. Grandma Jean, my dad's mother." When she looked back at the screen, RJ's eyes had softened.

"She was an amazing woman," said RJ, "very patient and kind. I would go over to her house when I

71

was a little girl and she would read books to me, then ask me what I thought about the story. Sometimes she asked what I wanted to be when I grew up. She would ask me about my day and what I was learning, what I was interested in. I don't remember her saying much apart from that, but I do remember how she listened. Grandma was a woman of few words, but I always felt she loved and appreciated me for who I was.

"My dad and even my mom probably thought they listened to me. But just about every conversation we had was about work and the company, and Dad always had to have the last word. I don't think I ever felt what you just said—seen, heard, and loved—when I talked to them. I'd like to think someday I might feel again the way I felt with Grandma Jean."

RJ sat up straighter. "My dad definitely listened in Level One," she said. "He was always right. I may have been young, but I had some good ideas. He never listened to me, though. So I understand the difference in how that kind of listening works, for sure. I guess I learned by watching my dad's example that Level One listening was the way to run this business."

Sophia nodded. "And you also have experience with Level Two and Level Three listening from your Grandma Jean. If someone listens to you in Level Two, you feel supported and acknowledged. When someone goes even deeper and dips into Level Three, bringing their full presence and intuition to the conversation, well, it's a beautiful human connection, and we're all wired to thrive with that kind of connection. The challenge for us these days is that most people connect with our thumbs through texting and social media posts, which isn't even *approaching* Level One. It's more like Level 0.5!"

"True enough," said RJ, laughing.

"We can do something to remedy that, though," said Sophia. "We need to recognize the emotional toll it takes on people, the isolation and loneliness they experience, when no one is deeply listening to them. And that's something you can definitely control, RJ— the way you listen to others."

Sophia had an idea, but she knew she needed to check with RJ first. "Are you up for experimenting with another baby step?"

"Actually," said RJ, "I'm feeling really tense right now. Look, I just noticed my hands are balled up like this." She held up her fists for Sophia to see. "This stuff is pretty far out of my comfort zone. But I'll try."

Sophia slowed her pace as she said gently, "Let's take a few deep breaths together and maybe you can let your hands relax a bit."

Sophia invited RJ to relax and led her through three very slow and deep breaths. She noticed RJ's shoulders relaxing. "Nice, RJ. How are you feeling now?"

RJ nodded. "Yes, that's better."

Sophia continued, "To experiment with the Levels of Listening, I recommend starting with the easiest conversations, with people you have a positive relationship with. Water runs along the path of least resistance, and that's a good metaphor to apply when you're learning a new skill. You can begin where there's the least resistance and work up from there. Is there a trusted person you could practice with, someone you could see yourself listening to at Level Two and Level Three?"

"I could practice it with my executive assistant, Maria. I've really come to rely on her to listen to me. And I often listen to her, too. At least I hope I do. I can let down my guard a little more with her."

"Excellent," said Sophia. "I encourage you to start there. And remember, when you become more aware of what you *don't* like and *don't* want, it is a step in the direction of creating what you *do* want. What I mean is, when you catch yourself listening at Level One, listening for problems to solve or looking for a way to be right, don't despair! That just means you're becoming more aware of your habit. As soon as you catch yourself in Level One, notice what you're thinking and feeling. Then take a breath, relax, and focus on the other person."

"Whew, I'm glad you said that," said RJ, "because I know Level One is my normal way of listening. And I think I tend to be hard on myself when I don't get things right the first time. The idea of noticing my bad habits makes me a little nervous. I think I have protected myself from looking at those too much, on the theory that ignorance is bliss.

"In fact," RJ said, "this scene just popped into my head: It's like I'm living alone in a castle, surrounded by a muddy moat. If I lower the drawbridge, I have no idea what will happen. So, I can't get out, and I can't seem to let anybody else in, either."

Sophia held the silence and was on the edge of her chair, leaning in to listen deeply as RJ shared such a powerful and frightening metaphor.

RJ let out a ragged sigh. "I've gotten used to being on my own in this stuffy castle, I guess. Letting down the drawbridge scares the dickens out of me. That moat could be full of alligators!"

"That's a pretty scary metaphor, RJ," said Sophia. "Being locked in a castle, surrounded by a moat full of alligators!" Hearing it, Sophia realized she needed to remember that coaching felt like risky territory for RJ, that exploring new ways of relating to herself and others was profoundly uncomfortable for her. Sophia wondered if modifying that metaphor might be useful to RJ.

"In our next session we can revisit that metaphor, if you are open to it, and see if a shift in visuals would support your journey. I sense that you know the journey is worth it, or you wouldn't be willing to experiment with these new exercises."

RJ nodded. "Yes, I hope it's worth it. And I am willing, for now."

"Well, our time is up today," said Sophia. "We have our next session in the calendar, so I look forward to seeing you then. As a way to complete our time together, would you be willing to share what was most valuable for you today?"

RJ thought for a moment. "I want to be seen, heard, and loved. I want to be seen, and I guess appreciated, for who I really am, not for what someone else thinks I should be. The trouble is, I don't think I really *know* who I am yet." RJ took a deep breath. "Well, thanks for today, Sophia."

"My pleasure, RJ," said Sophia. "You're doing big work."

# 6

## Is Something Bothering You?

Sophia got up from her desk and walked out the door of her home office to take a break. She plopped down on the couch and gazed out the living room window. Earlier this morning the room had been flooded with sunlight. Now it had turned shadowy and gray. From the open window she caught a whiff of rain. Soon the showers would be nourishing her yard and flowerpots. Before moving to the Pacific Northwest over thirty years ago, Sophia had expected near-constant rains. Now a full-fledged Northwesterner, she appreciated nature's balance of rainy and dry days, light and shadow—a perfect recipe for the extraordinary beauty of this part of the world.

"All right, Sophia, time to get back to work," she said to herself, rising from the couch and returning to her office. She sat down at the red desk. Seeing that cheery color always brightened her attitude and gave her a little boost of energy. She opened her laptop. There was a new email from RJ with the subject line "Update."

"What could this be? Surely RJ's not quitting coaching already," Sophia mused as she opened the email.

*Dear Sophia,*

*I am writing to share an experience I had this morning with Maria and the 3 levels of listening—my homework, remember? Every Friday morning Maria prepares a detailed calendar for my upcoming week, complete with background on who I am meeting with, the reading materials for each appointment, driving instructions if it is an out-of-the-office meeting, etc. In other words, it is a big project for Maria each week.*

*This morning Maria went over next week's schedule with me. I listened, as I usually do, for scheduling glitches and for details that Maria sometimes gets wrong. Either she schedules too little or too much time, omits the reading material, doesn't allow me enough travel time, or introduces some other problem that throws my day into turmoil. But then I remembered my homework to practice the 3 levels of listening. I only remembered the first one, which you called "listening to be right," and realized that was exactly what I was doing. I was listening for Maria's mistakes, to show her that I was right and she was wrong. I don't know why I caught myself, but I did. (That's progress, right?) I can't remember what the second type of listening was, but it felt like I listened differently once I realized what I was doing.*

*I was surprised at what else happened: Maria likes to include what she calls "RJ time" for me to have a little space in my day and slow down. She's tried to sneak in those time segments before and I always tell her to fill them with appointments. This morning when I stopped listening for problems and ways to be right, I suddenly saw "RJ time" a little differently. I had never allowed myself to consider that maybe I deserved some "RJ time." The result: I didn't fight her on it this time and we left two blocks of "RJ time" in the schedule for next week. I simply said, "Thank you, Maria. This looks good." I'm not sure, but I think I noticed a little smile on her face as I headed back to my office, plus I didn't feel like I had just finished a boxing match. We didn't get into the usual tussle over my schedule this time. Anyway, I wanted to report to you on my homework. See you at our next appointment.*

*Best,*

*RJ*

Sophia beamed. She reread the email. "It's moments like this that make a coach's day," she thought, then wondered, "Should I send a reply now or wait awhile? I don't want to give RJ the impression I sit here all day waiting for her emails. I don't want to look overeager."

Sophia reflected for a moment, checking in with herself. "There's really nothing to resist or push away here. There's no one to please." She took a deep breath and wrote a brief reply.

*Dear RJ,*

*Thanks for sharing this story and your insights. Nice job on the homework. I too look forward to our next session. See you then.*

*Take good care,*

*Sophia*

Sophia heard a soft pattering sound from outside. The gentle sprinkle had turned to a summer shower. She got up to close the window, drinking in a full breath of moist, fresh air, then returned to her desk.

Ping! Her tablet signaled an incoming video call. "What a nice surprise, Tara," Sophia said as she positioned her tablet so she could see Tara's beautiful face.

Sophia had emailed Tara the week before: "I'm trying to decide on a quote for Gabe's birthday mug. Any suggestions?" She knew Gabe would appreciate having a special coffee mug as well as the treat she planned to enclose along with it—a gift certificate from his favorite sports equipment store in Boulder, Colorado, where he was now living and working.

"I got your email last week asking me if I had a suggestion for a special quote to go on Gabe's birthday coffee mug," Tara said, smiling. "Nothing came to mind right away, and I realized this morning I had forgotten to get back to you. The old brain isn't as quick as it used to be." Tara laughed. "Hope you weren't waiting on me."

"Thanks for checking in. I didn't want to be late for his birthday, so I shipped the mug yesterday," Sophia said with a subdued tone in her voice. "No worries."

Gabe, Sophia's only child, took a gap year after high school and moved to Colorado to ski for the winter and fish in the summer. When one year turned into four, Sophia started to worry that her son might not go on to college. Her fears were unfounded, however. Gabe had earned his digital design degree at a Colorado community college, even figuring out how to pay his own way. Soon after, he got hired as the web designer for the Boulder-based company that manufactured his favorite skis. Now he served on the company's innovations team.

When Gabe left for Colorado, he had shared with Sophia his desire to make a good living doing something that balanced his commitment to a healthy environment and doing what he loved. No surprise that the outdoor outfitter wanted to hire him—he had always loved skiing, fishing, and spending time in the mountains. The job was a perfect match.

In the photo collage on Sophia's living room coffee table was a picture of Gabe standing atop a snowy peak, looking into the sunset with a pensive gaze. That beautiful photo, taken by one of his hiking pals, always reminded Sophia of the time Gabe had said he hoped he could make decisions based upon "seven generations hence," an Indigenous way of living that he had learned. He had often talked with deep concern about the impact of climate change on future generations.

Sophia loved creating unique gifts for Gabe's birthday that were both practical and fun. She had found an online company that specialized in printing quotes on mugs and reached out to Tara for her advice. But before Tara called, she had found a quote she liked and had already ordered the mug.

Tara asked, "How are you, Sophia? How's it going with your new client?"

"Thanks for asking. I think it's going okay. In fact, I just got an email from her this morning sharing a story about how she listened differently in a meeting with her executive assistant. So far, she's embracing the learning, but who knows what may happen when she gets busier."

Tara leaned in toward the camera and held Sophia's gaze for a moment that seemed like an eternity. "Just curious," she said softly. "While we were chatting about Gabe's mug, I noticed a shortness in your voice. You seemed lost in thought. Just wondering—is something bothering you?" Tara asked.

Sophia flushed with uneasiness. How was it that Tara always seemed to pick up the subtleties in Sophia's energy, even on a video call? She was a master at Level Three Listening—listening with her intuition. It was what she most admired about Tara—her potent presence. She had a capacity to speak her truth directly, yet always with kindness. Over the fifteen years since they had first met, Sophia had learned to trust her friend's hunches. If Tara was picking up something in Sophia that seemed off-balance, it was worth looking into.

"Okay, Tara. Let me check in with myself for a moment. I have felt a little off for the last day or two, and I am not exactly sure what's going on. At first, I thought it was the rain, the change to gray weather, because that often affects my mood, but I think it is deeper than that," said Sophia. "Let me be still for a moment and reflect." She closed her eyes and took a few deep breaths, unconcerned about rushing. She had known Tara long enough to trust that she appreciated meaningful silence.

At last Sophia said, "It's Gabe's birthday, I think. His birthday can be a stressful time for me."

Thinking back, Sophia recalled the first time she had met Tara, walking on the beach near the Olympia Peninsula. Sophia had just divorced her husband, Dan, and had driven out to the beach for a personal retreat and some much-needed rest.

Sophia had originally been attracted to Dan's strong personality and confident style. But it didn't take long for the cracks to show in their connection. Then when Gabe arrived and they became a family, significant differences in their parenting philosophies soon became apparent. On Gabe's third birthday, she and Dan had invited a few friends over to celebrate. Gabe was so excited to greet his friends that he ran down their steep driveway and fell hard, face forward on the cement, cutting his little hands and bloodying his knees and face. Instead of rushing to Gabe and comforting him as Sophia did, Dan stood back and yelled, "Get up, Gabe, and don't cry, either. We have guests. You have to learn to be a man. Time to get tough—let's go!"

After the party Sophia sat in the bathroom, crying alone, realizing that while she was aware of her husband's growing coldness toward her, she hadn't realized it could also pierce Gabe's young heart. Learning to live without their emotional connection as husband and wife was taking a toll, but in that moment, she saw that her son's psychological safety was also at risk.

After that day, similar incidents frightened Sophia. She compensated, coming up with excuses for Dan's distant behavior as a parent and husband. She even tried to overlook his brief infidelity, hoping to keep the family together. But the turning point came when Gabe was nine years old. He loved baseball and playing on a Little League team. During one game, Gabe struck out with the bases loaded and ran back to the dugout, embarrassed and tearful. Dan jumped down out of the stands and marched into the dugout, pulled Gabe aside by his collar, and yelled at him to stop crying. He shook Gabe's shoulders so hard that Sophia was stunned, fearing Dan might be hurting far more than Gabe's feelings.

After that incident Sophia talked to Dan about the importance of supporting Gabe and being loving toward him when he felt sad, instead of belittling and shaming him. In a mean-spirited outburst Dan yelled that Sophia "had better get used to it" because they were heading into Gabe's teen years and Dan was not going to tolerate any "bad behavior."

Seeing Dan's lack of remorse, Sophia began to face the truth—she was dying inside. The persecuting criticisms and verbal abuse were becoming more intense and frequent. Once outgoing, Sophia gradually withdrew from friends. At work she kept to herself, and when asked to lead a new team initiative, she looked for ways to disengage and supported others to lead it instead.

One evening, while Dan was on a business trip, she and Gabe had a fun evening together, watching a movie on the kids' channel, eating popcorn, laughing and being silly. When she tucked Gabe into bed and kissed him good night, Gabe asked when his daddy was coming home. When Sophia said Daddy would be back in a few days, Gabe had laid his head in her lap and softly cried, saying, "Sometimes Daddy scares me."

That night Sophia went to bed praying for the courage to face the painful truth about her marriage and the impact Dan's anger was having on their son. The next morning, she packed clothes for Gabe and a few things for herself and drove to her parents' house to stay until she decided what to do. The part of Sophia that had been willing to endure so much to maintain a home and family was the same fierce part of her that would do whatever it took to ensure that her son was safe to grow and thrive.

A few months later Sophia filed for divorce. Since Dan traveled almost full-time, it was agreed Sophia would have primary custody of Gabe. Facing the uncertainty of being a single parent was painful, but Sophia felt a profound relief knowing she had opted for a safe space for herself and her son.

Now Gabe was twenty-four years old, a young man, thriving in Colorado doing work that he loved and enjoying a renewed connection with his dad. That time in her life as a young parent was now a distant but still difficult memory. Designing Gabe's birthday mug brought it all back to Sophia as though it were only yesterday.

Returning to the point, Sophia opened her eyes and said, "Tara, you are right. Somehow that awful memory of Gabe's third birthday party is still with me, lodged deep in my bones. While I know he is safe and doing fine now, those old pictures got kicked up in my mind. When I get scared, I stand back and disengage. Feeling powerless in the face of all those old memories, I end up hiding, the way I once hid from the truth of the abuse. Even now, I still feel the need to protect myself from hurt and disappointment."

"That was a painful time," said Tara. "It is understandable that you'd still have sad memories." Sophia felt tears welling up.

Tara continued, "Being a protective parent was a role you had to take on, and it was completely appropriate for that time. The protector in you stepped forward when your son needed you. But I understand why the sadness of that time still comes back to you, even now that Gabe is a wonderful young man and doing so well on his own. Sophia, we have many different parts inside us. Gradually we learn to honor all of those parts with none left out. We do the best we can, you know." She smiled.

"I have tried not to feel like a Victim to that time in my life. I don't want to be distant or superficial with people, especially not with you, my friend. I want to be trusting, hopeful, and engaged," said Sophia.

Sophia blinked and looked away, then began again. "The struggles in my marriage and disappointments from old work engagements that I had high hopes for—those have stayed with me. I know I'm still upset about that president who cancelled the yearlong coaching program four years ago. I gave the company my very best self, and what happened? He cancelled the whole project without so much as a conversation. I felt tossed aside. It was another example of how, when I get excited about something I want, I become nice and easy to get along with, hoping it will turn out. But inside I'm afraid that disappointment is lurking just around the corner. I stay vigilant, worried about others and what they might do, often swallowing my voice so as not to rock the boat. 'Smile and be nice,' I often heard at home growing up."

Tara spoke slowly. "We're all on a journey to embrace the totality of who we are as human beings. And the part of us we don't want to accept is a window to what we most want in life. You would not have become protective unless you really cared about something. I sense that what you most wanted for yourself and your son was love, intimacy, and connection."

She continued, "I also know how much you want to make a positive difference in the world, and you do that by coaching influential leaders. That is important to you."

Sophia felt the power of the moment. Silently she repeated Tara's words to herself: "The part of us we don't want to accept is a window to what we most want in life."

"You asked about my new client," said Sophia. "*She's* an influential community leader. In our last session she described herself as living in her personal castle guarded by a moat full of alligators. I don't want to live in my protective castle, either, Tara, but I see now that sometimes I do close off. I have my own persistent ways of protecting myself from getting hurt."

"Our wounds stay with us in some form no matter how long we live on this earth," said Tara. "It's how we relate to them that matters, though. We always have a choice to struggle against our human journey or accept and appreciate the wonder in it."

Sophia let a silence settle over them like a warm blanket, wrapped around them, holding their loving relationship. "Tara, you're facing a difficult time also, knowing how your brother's disease is progressing. Don't you worry about Paco?"

"Many things can happen or go wrong in life," said Tara. "The question is not whether bad things will happen. They will. The purpose of life is to enjoy this mysterious experience, with all its joys and pains. We were not put on this earth just to suffer. The fact is, we were born, and we will die. During the in-between time we have a choice: whether to enjoy and appreciate the experience or resent it because it can bring pain. Paco and I love each other very much and we have enjoyed our life together. Yes, I am sad to see his health deteriorating. I still choose to see life as a beautiful experience. Events don't determine whether or not I'm happy. I do."

# 7

## The Dreaded Drama Triangle

Hello, RJ," said Sophia as her client's face appeared on the tablet screen. In the background was a large, colorful landscape print depicting a trio of boats with bright sails drifting past an array of mountains.

"Is that a new piece of artwork on your office wall?"

"Nice, isn't it? I took the 'RJ time' that Maria scheduled for me. It was only a few hours, but still . . . one step forward in the name of self-care," said RJ with pride. "I went to a local art gallery and bought that print. Maria hung it for me.

"It brightens up this place," RJ added. "Something to look at besides the usual construction documents and other paperwork."

"I like it," said Sophia. "And congratulations on taking some RJ time. What was that like, treating yourself to some personal time off?"

RJ made a distressed face and pulled her head back. "Pretty uncomfortable at first. I kept checking my phone, reading emails and texts. But I've been noticing a new art gallery near my condo for months now, so I decided to go and check it out. I had so many emails on my phone that I almost didn't go in. I couldn't help answering a few, but when I stepped into the gallery, they asked me to put my phone away so I couldn't take any pictures. It was hard at first, but since it was their rule, I just went with it. Not sure I would have set that boundary for myself otherwise. When I left the gallery and checked my phone again, I had surprisingly few new emails. So, I went to dinner at a little bistro nearby, had a glass of wine, and really enjoyed myself. It was one of those classically gorgeous Northwest evenings. Anyway, that was when I bought the print."

"That's great. And now you have a piece of artwork to remind you of that relaxing time.

"RJ," Sophia continued, "I received your email about trying out the Three Levels of Listening. Any other insights you'd like to share about that?"

"Yes, actually. When I tried the Three Levels of Listening with Maria, I think it made a difference in our conversation. That felt really good. But it is a lot harder to do with other people. I mainly noticed how much I listen in Level One—listening to be right—and then, how I started criticizing myself when I noticed that."

"Good catch, RJ. The urge to judge what we hear as being either good or bad is common for most of us," said Sophia. "While the other person's talking, we often ask ourselves, 'Do I agree or disagree?' We tend to look for opportunities to jump in and share our viewpoint. That creates a barrier to open communication and learning together.

"If we like what the other person is saying, we get excited. If we don't, well, we may get defensive, dogmatic, or critical, and feel a lot of heavy emotions that stop us from connecting with the person speaking. It's practically impossible to listen with all that internal noise!" said Sophia.

Sophia went on. "At times like that, I'll often ask myself, 'Do I want to connect or convince?' It's a reflective question you may want to experiment with. That question is especially useful when you're about to engage in a conversation where it may be hard to listen.

"Most often, if I stop to ask myself that question, I can readily see that I really do want to connect, and that helps clarify my intention. But if I answer, 'No, I want to convince them and be right!' it stops me in my tracks and jolts me back to reflect a bit."

"I think I *will* use that question," said RJ. "What was it again? 'Do I want to connect or convince?' That's good. But I'm guessing I'll probably want to convince a lot more often than I want to connect." She grimaced. "I didn't realize how much I want to 'win the point,' as you say, until I practiced those levels of listening."

"It does take practice," said Sophia. "It may help to remember that when you listen in Levels Two and Three, it invites others to share more openly, because they sense you actually want to hear what they have to say. That can begin to create the trust you're wanting to foster. In an environment of trust, people can feel safe enough to contribute the kinds of ideas that keep a company up to date.

"As you listen at those deeper levels to what the other person is sharing, the questions you ask naturally arise from the information they're offering you. That's when an authentic connection begins. It's also an opportunity to develop the skill of curiosity—

so important for any leader seeking to cultivate innovation and critical thinking. Of course, we're talking about a *friendly* curiosity here, not a *probing* curiosity," Sophia added.

RJ frowned a little. "Friendly curiosity or probing curiosity? What's the difference?"

"When you think of a friendly curiosity, what comes up for you?" asked Sophia.

"Well," said RJ, "like I would sit down and really listen to a friend, I guess. Like when my Grandma Jean used to say, 'I really need a good listening-to!' I've always remembered her saying that—maybe I was a little surprised as a kid that even my grandmother needed a listening ear. For someone to just sit with her and hear whatever she wanted to talk about."

RJ continued, "I have only a couple of good friends I can do that with. And I don't do it very often! The idea of friendly curiosity sounds really nice. I certainly remember how good it felt when Grandma Jean simply listened to me. I'd sit at her kitchen table and we'd just talk while she cooked. When I was with her, I felt important."

"That's beautiful, RJ," said Sophia. "Your Grandma Jean's kitchen sounds like a very soothing, dare I say loving, environment. That's the kind of environment where friendly curiosity thrives.

"Probing curiosity has a different tone," said Sophia. "It is forceful and sometimes even a little harsh. As though the person asking questions is looking for a specific response. You are curious because you are probing to get the 'right answer.'"

"Hmm. Can you give me an example?" RJ asked.

Sophia thought for a moment. "Let's say Maria shares with you one afternoon that she's not feeling well. Friendly curiosity might sound like this: 'Maria, I'm sorry to hear that. What do you need to take care of yourself?' You would ask with a friendly, curious tone, asking Maria to discern what is in her best interest. You're leaving the power with her to reveal what she needs.

"Probing curiosity is similar but has a different tone and intention. It might sound like this: 'Maria, I'm sorry to hear that. What work needs to get done so that you can go home?' This is probing curiosity— your focus is on Maria getting her work done and reporting that plan to you *before* considering what she may need. You've kept the power with you. Friendly curiosity lets go of control . . . and probing curiosity can be a subtle way of maintaining control."

"Okay," RJ said, nodding. "I think I get the difference. Another thing for me to try, I guess."

"How you listen will have everything to do with how you relate to others and to circumstances. Do you remember the FISBE we talked about? It describes the profound idea that we humans have an operating system that starts with a thought or focus and then, depending on the intensity and nature of the thought, an emotion arises—our inner state—in response to that thought. Remember all that?"

"Yes, that has stayed with me . . . because it rhymes with Frisbee." RJ smiled.

"I am going to share my screen and bring up the whiteboard." Sophia paused to locate the settings on the video platform that would let her draw the triangle diagram onscreen.

"Can you see this triangle on the whiteboard, RJ?"

"Yes, I can see it."

"Oh good." Sophia continued, "I think what your colleague Roger, who referred you to me, liked about this triangle diagram is that it helped him feel normal. What I mean by that is that this triangle represents the three primary ways we human beings normally respond when we feel uncomfortable emotions, which can trigger our reactive habits.

"I'll take a few minutes to explain this triangle diagram. I'd like you to consider how it can help you understand and manage your anxiety when it threatens to derail you—when it threatens to stop you from deeply listening," Sophia said.

"Over the last few decades psychologists who studied human behavior observed three universal ways that we human beings respond to uncomfortable situations.* All are 'normal' responses to that discomfort.

"One way we respond is to feel sorry for ourselves and believe we're powerless in the face of whatever we see as being the problem. When this happens, we feel incapable, or even hopeless, about resolving the situation, or ever having what we want. We may complain and avoid taking responsibility for our actions and choices. Then we often look for someone or something to blame for our situation. That type of behavior and thinking describes the Victim role in the Drama Triangle." Sophia pointed to the bottom of the inverted triangle diagram.

"I heard you when you said earlier that you hate the word *victim*," she added, "and I can understand why. It's not an enjoyable role to be playing." Sophia paused to see if RJ wanted to say anything, but she seemed content to listen.

"Before we go on, I want to share a very important difference between victimization and victimhood. Everyone at some point is likely to experience being victimized. It may be a disease, loss of work, being victimized by a crime, or simply getting cut off in traffic by a fast driver. These are situations where we have no control, and they are things that happen from outside us. Victimhood, on the other hand, comes from inside us. It is a way of relating to what happens in life when we believe we have no choice. We become Victims to our own thinking, confined by the limitations of our own mind, which is the hallmark of victimhood."

"I have to think about this for a moment, but, actually," RJ said, "I think I understand what you mean."

"Is it okay with you if I continue by describing the other two roles?" asked Sophia.

"Sure," said RJ.

Sophia continued, "By the way, the message we often say to ourselves when we're caught in the Victim role is 'Poor me' or 'Why me?' She drew a sad face emoji on the digital whiteboard.

"The second role that shows up to manage our uncomfortable feelings," said Sophia, "is the Persecutor." She wrote *Persecutor* and *It's all your fault* at the upper right corner of the triangle.

"When we're operating in this role, we adopt a more controlling, aggressive strategy against whatever is happening. Fearful of becoming a Victim, in the Persecutor role we try to control the situation and assign blame. The Persecutor's motto is 'It's all your fault.' From the Victim's point of view, however, the Persecutor, whether it's a person or situation, is the 'problem.'"

Sophia added, "Once the struggle begins, between the Victim saying, 'Poor me,' and the Persecutor saying, 'It's all your fault,' then this third role steps in." Sophia pointed to the upper left corner of the triangle. "The Rescuer says, 'You poor things. Let me help.'"

"Sounds like the Rescuer wants to be the hero," RJ interjected.

"Yes, exactly!" said Sophia. "The Rescuer is like the hero in every fairy tale—or in any movie you've seen or novel you've read. The Rescuer is the helper, or the pain reliever, who wants everyone to just get along and avoid conflict. Focused on the needs of everyone else, the Rescuer ignores their own needs and becomes overly pleasing and accommodating. This may sound nice on the surface, and it's certainly culturally acceptable—everyone likes people who are helpful, right? But being stuck in the Rescuer role is a recipe for burnout and exhaustion. The Rescuer seeks to take care of everyone else but with hardly a clue about how to take care of themselves."

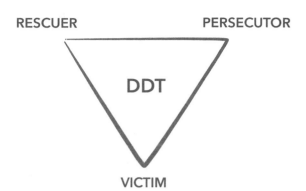

*Diagram 2. Dreaded Drama Triangle (DDT)*

"So, to sum all this up," said Sophia, "the Dreaded Drama Triangle, or DDT, as I call it, like the poison, represents the three ways we humans manage our uncomfortable emotions when we focus on what we don't like and don't want. Depending on the type of reaction we have, here's how each of the three roles work." Sophia left the whiteboard and clicked to pull up a PowerPoint slide, and continued.

"When we move *away* from the uncomfortable emotions, we withdraw and feel powerless. This aligns with the Victim role.

"When we move *against* the emotions and situations and seek to aggressively control the situation, our reaction aligns with the Persecutor role.

"When we move *toward, or lean in*, to be helpful, seeking to soothe or please, that reaction aligns with the Rescuer role.

"All three roles are simply strategies to help us navigate uncomfortable feelings in the moment. The difficulty occurs when these are the only way we have of working with unpleasant moments—then we get stuck racing around the Drama Triangle, caught in a cycle of reactivity."

RJ stared at the screen, nodding, taking in the points. "It's pretty clear which one I am."

"Oh? Which one stands out for you?"

"Isn't it obvious? I am the Persecutor. I detest people who play the Victim, and I've aggressively built up this company to where it is today. I'm the leader so I tend to dominate conversations, and I work very hard to keep things under control. I was taught that's the way to succeed in this industry. I think Dad would be very proud of me, in fact."

"Okay," said Sophia, taking it all in. "I noticed you said, 'I am the Persecutor.' I want to be clear, RJ, that these roles are ways of behaving. They're not *who you are*; they're not your essence as a human being. They are only roles we take on—like characters in a play or novel. The roles describe different ways we try to do our best to cope with all the challenges life throws at us. Language is important here. Do you see the difference?"

"What do you suggest, then? That I say, 'I am playing the role of a Persecutor'?" RJ retorted. "That sounds ridiculous."

Sophia smiled. "Actually, yes. Because it's a role and not a character judgment. You and I, and all human beings, *play* these roles at times. This diagram can be helpful in considering your patterns, how you tend to react when you feel you're in a tight spot.

*Psychologist Dr. Karen Horney in the 1940s condensed human behavior into three categories that align with the Drama Triangle roles: The first behavior is compliance and moving toward people; the second is moving against people or aggression; and the third is the need to move away, or withdraw.

"In another session I'll share with you the second triangle diagram, one that describes the three positive alternatives to these roles. It's called The Empowerment Dynamic and it describes us when we're at our best, living as our best self. But that is for later.

"We've covered a lot today," said Sophia. "Let's pause, take a few deep breaths, and check in. How does that sound?"

"That sounds fine. Sure." RJ closed her eyes and breathed deeply and let out a long sigh. She opened her eyes. "Okay, what's next?"

Sophia smiled, noticing how quickly RJ snapped out of the moment of reflection and deep breathing. "Her urge to act quickly runs deep," Sophia thought to herself.

"There's no rush, RJ. We have a few more minutes. Go ahead and take another deep breath or two. Deep breathing helps the body de-stress and naturally restore itself. It's a valuable skill all by itself."

"Okay," said RJ, sounding doubtful. She took another deep breath and let it go. "I don't think I usually breathe very deeply. To tell you the truth, it feels a little weird."

"That's okay," encouraged Sophia. "As you continue doing it, breathing fully will come more naturally. Are you open to pausing a few times during the day, just to take a few deep breaths, and see if it gets easier?"

RJ nodded with a bit of a smirk on her face. "Sure, okay. So now I'm going to become a breathing expert, eh?"

Sophia laughed. "You may not become an expert, but you'll probably notice that you become more relaxed, generally. I call it taking a Three Breath Break. I encourage you to give it a try.

"RJ, between now and the next time we talk, I invite you to consider these roles that make up the Drama Triangle. See if, as you consider these roles, you become more aware of any habits of thinking that may keep you in the grip of the DDT.

"At the same time, it's important to remember," Sophia added, "that our intention here is not to demonize or try to fix any part of you. What we *are* after is to simply observe first, and respect the different parts of you—get really curious about their purpose. For example, when a DDT role emerges in your behavior, what need is that role meeting? Even though it may not always be helpful, it's trying to accomplish something, right? How might that role be trying to support you?

"When you do that kind of self-inquiry, do it with heaps of self-compassion. That's really the key!" Sophia smiled and waited for RJ to respond.

"You've given me lots to think about, Sophia." RJ sighed. "Here's the deal, though. I have a strong Persecutor role going on—I can see that. I mean, I know myself. What if I start persecuting myself for being a Persecutor?" RJ chuckled, but Sophia picked up a hint of sadness. RJ wanted, needed, encouragement to break out of her long-held patterns. Sophia was committed to giving her that support, but she also knew the real breakthroughs would come as RJ began to observe her reactive patterns with understanding and kindness.

"That's a great self-observation, RJ. Watch those roles wherever they come up and notice what you say to yourself. I encourage you to see these roles as normal, common to everyone. And now that you know about the DDT roles, believe me, you'll start to see them show up everywhere—in the news, advertisements, politics, conversations, even religion. The DDT is like a blueprint of the way we humans interact with other people and situations, even with ourselves."

RJ frowned a little. "Okay . . . "

"You'll get a look at a better blueprint when I show you The Empowerment Dynamic triangle and its positive roles of Creator, Challenger, and Coach next time we talk," Sophia said. "And remember that it's important to have lots of compassion for yourself and for others, too, as you watch these roles play out in life. Will you take that on as your homework?"

"I'll give it a shot," said RJ matter-of-factly.

Sophia nodded. "Good. As we wrap up here, is there anything else you want to say about today's session?"

"Wow," RJ said with a hint of sarcasm. "That's about all I can say. Working on how I listen to people, staying curious, and learning self-compassion for my persecuting ways. That's a lot. And I never thought that compassion would be part of this." She paused.

"Sometimes I don't think I have a compassionate bone in my body. That just wasn't something we ever talked about in my family. I wouldn't say it was encouraged."

"So, I just heard one of the DDT voices speaking," offered Sophia. "Did you hear it?"

"No!" RJ looked stunned. "What did I say?"

"What you said is you don't think you have a compassionate bone in your body. These DDT roles also operate inside of us, in the way we talk to ourselves. Which role might be saying, 'I don't have a compassionate bone in my body'?"

"Hmm," said RJ, a slight frown signaling she was taking in the fact that the DDT roles could be having an inside conversation. She nodded slowly.

"The Persecuter's voice? I am persecuting myself for not being compassionate. Is that right?"

"How does that land for you?" asked Sophia.

"How it lands is that I probably say things like that to myself all day long without realizing it. I mean, I did it just now and wouldn't have noticed it if you hadn't pointed it out," she said sadly.

"So, I really don't see how I'm going to catch these DDT roles in the act . . ." She looked at Sophia searchingly.

"It will get easier to spot them, I promise," Sophia said. "Just keep looking. I've found that most people are their own worst critics. In my own case, even after coaching hundreds of people over the last several years, the voice of my inner critic is still the one I hear most often. I call it my Inner Persecutor. It is a strong voice, but it rarely says anything truly helpful. None of us operates very well when someone's yelling at us— whether the yelling is coming from outside, or inside."

"It's a lot to think about!" exclaimed RJ.

"Yes, it is," agreed Sophia. "You've entered the doorway to becoming the person you want to be— your best self. And there's a lot to welcome."

RJ looked incredulous. "But how can listening to my Inner Persecutor be a doorway to my best self? Isn't hearing all its criticism just going to make me feel worse?"

"This is a really important question, RJ," said Sophia. "Actually, when you push your Inner Persecutor underground and resist listening to what it has to say, even becoming critical of it—persecuting *it*—that makes its voice grow stronger and louder. When you pause and listen to your internal dialogue, though, you can learn quite a lot.

"That part of you wants to be heard and seen," Sophia added. "I realize that may sound counterintuitive. It's natural to try to ignore that voice, and that's okay some of the time. But when it gets louder and stronger, try to pause and hear what it's *really* trying to say, behind the yelling. I trust that awareness will continue to unfold for you."

Sophia went on to say, "I am curious how you might have some fun with noticing and naming the DDT roles when they show up. Any idea how you could do that?"

RJ thought for a moment, then said, "I wish I had an app. Maria uses an app on her phone that helps her identify birds when she takes walks in the local parks—she's quite the bird-watcher. When she sees or hears a bird she doesn't recognize, she inputs its description, and the app identifies the bird and tells her more about its habitat. But I don't think you have an app that identifies drama roles, do you?" she said with a laugh. "But I guess I could use my Notes app to keep track of what I notice during the day. What did you call it, 'noticing and naming?'"

"I love that idea, RJ! That is so creative. Yes, I call it noticing and naming your roles as they surface. Go ahead and have fun with the process. You might record any messages you hear yourself or others say," Sophia recommended. "Each time you do that, you might ask yourself whether you're identifying more with the Victim, Persecutor, or Rescuer role in that moment."

"Okay," said RJ, "I'll try that. Even though I don't know what I'm doing."

"Go slow. Give yourself a break and keep at it," urged Sophia. "Listening for all the DDT roles can yield amazing insights if you can listen with some kindness toward yourself.

"We'll go deeper into this next time. Your homework until then, RJ, is to continue to listen with compassion. Get really curious about your inner voices, find out what they're saying, and notice and name them on your phone—you're not pushing them away, but welcoming them. As you do that, you may be surprised how much you learn from them."

RJ frowned, then wrinkled her upper lip and scrunched her nose to make a silly face.

Sophia laughed. "It sounds a little paradoxical, I know."

"Okay, I'll try to listen to myself with less judgment and a little more fun, but this is new territory for me. I guess if I can listen to Maria in Level Two, then maybe I can learn to listen to myself."

"With compassion!" Sophia reminded her.

"I'll try. No guarantees, though. Thanks. Gotta run."

"See you next time, RJ," said Sophia, waving as she signed off.

# 8

## The Inner DDT

After the session with RJ, Sophia walked to her favorite neighborhood café. She was ready for a leisurely afternoon lunch outside on the patio and an opportunity to journal about her recent coaching session with RJ.

Treating herself to a long break, slowing down, and getting quiet for a few moments was now one of Sophia's most treasured simple pleasures. She had once thought she needed to take vacation time or schedule an expensive massage and spa day to give herself the self-care she required. But while those experiences were enjoyable, they often left Sophia wanting more private personal time afterward. Nowadays, though, she knew how important it was to take a few contemplative moments—even if it was only for fifteen minutes a day—to intentionally go inward and pay attention to whatever she noticed inside. Doing this daily renewed her spirit. Buoyed by this practice, she found she was more resilient and in turn had greater capacity to show up as her best self and to be of real service.

Now, sitting outside at the café, Sophia's intention was to reflect on her session with RJ, as well as to journal about a recent experience she had the previous Sunday. A familiar server approached her table with a warm greeting and asked, "Will you be having your usual?"

Pleased by the personal connection, Sophia said, "Yes, thank you. It's kind of you to remember."

He scribbled on his notepad. "I'll go put that in for you!" he said, then headed off to the kitchen.

Sophia reached into her bag, took out her journal and pen, and began writing. To her surprise, the first sentence she wrote was RJ's statement: *I don't have a compassionate bone in my body.* She found it helped to write down these key statements by her clients. Putting them on paper, Sophia was able to give them further thought.

*What a demeaning thing to say about oneself,* she wrote. *If one of RJ's employees said that to her, I reckon she would be furious and quick to defend herself.*

She continued, *What is it about us human beings that makes us speak critically and cruelly to ourselves? The DDT roles are so helpful in getting me to observe how I'm relating to other people or situations. And it was useful for RJ, too, to see her Inner Persecutor showing up in the form of that harsh self-criticism. In fact, the DDT is one of the most useful ideas I have to share with clients, because the triangle diagram and the simplicity of the three roles is "sticky." It stays with them and helps awaken their inner observer.*

She paused a moment. Where had that phrase come from? "Awaken the inner observer" had seemed to pop up out of nowhere. And yet it was so apt.

*I like that,* wrote Sophia. *'Awakening the inner observer' really describes what happens when we look within. When we can pause, notice, and name the roles, it helps us to get distance from them. And the proof is in the pudding. Clients do say it helps them feel less stuck. It helps me, too. Once I notice and name the roles, I get some relief. I don't feel as overwhelmed or baffled by whatever is occurring in the moment. At the same time, when I am in the middle of something challenging, I can easily forget the grip the DDT roles have on me. Those roles operate inside me, too, not just outwardly. How I relate to myself is just as important as how I relate to others.*

Sophia paused and read over what she had written. "My job is to weaken the grip the DDT has on me and strengthen my inner observer," she thought. "Maybe that's the formula that leads me out of the DDT? Observing inwardly, how I'm relating to *myself*," Sophia reflected. "That really is the biggest question, isn't it?"

The server set down a glass of sparkling water and Sophia smiled her appreciation. She took a refreshing sip and returned to her journal.

She wrote, *The DDT roles are so helpful for looking at how I relate to others. But how about how I relate to myself? Seems as if RJ was in the Persecutor role when she criticized herself for not having a compassionate bone in her body.*

The notion of an "internal DDT triangle" had been on Sophia's mind since the previous Sunday. As she walked down her favorite street, she had realized that all three of the DDT roles—Victim, Persecutor, and Rescuer—operated inside of her without any obvious influence from outer events. She wrote,

*Last Sunday's walk: a beautiful summer day. I walked along Olympic View Road, appreciating that gorgeous view of the water and mountains, but feeling a little bit down. The neighborhood is known for its large, elegant homes with stylish landscaped yards and spectacular views. As I admired those beautiful homes, a loud, critical voice inside my head said, "Why do you come out here for a walk? You just upset yourself because you know you will never have a garden or a home like one of these. You should go back home and walk in your own neighborhood!"*

*I stopped in my tracks. It was shocking to hear such a demeaning voice coming from within. But then suddenly I heard another voice saying, "She's right. Go back home so you don't get yourself more upset than you already are."*

*It seemed best to obey those strong voices, so I turned around. But as I headed back to the parking lot to go home, I felt like a Victim to my own thinking!*

Sophia took a sip of her water. She could feel herself getting upset all over again, thinking of that experience. "Astonishing," she thought. "To hear the different DDT roles inside myself, talking to each other!"

She took a deep breath and looked up for a moment, grateful to be taking the time to process the experience. Suddenly she had an idea. "I think I'll map this experience through the DDT framework."

Sophia drew a downward-pointed triangle and wrote *Inner Victim* at the bottom. Next to it she wrote: *I feel powerless to attain my dream of having a large, beautiful garden.*

Then at the upper right corner of the triangle she wrote *Inner Persecutor*. Next to that she wrote, *Why do you come out here, anyway? You just make yourself feel bad.*

She paused to look at the drawing. "Wow, this is fascinating! But now, what was the Rescuer voice saying?"

In the upper left corner of the triangle, Sophia wrote *Inner Rescuer*. Next to it she added, *You'll feel better if you just go home.*

"My pain reliever, right on cue," she thought. "Amazing. I was playing all three roles with myself in that one internal conversation. No one was talking to me. It was just me, talking to myself. The weather was idyllic. The yards and flowers were just as beautiful as ever. In one short series of thoughts, I convinced myself that I was a Victim to my own Inner Persecutor and immediately allowed my Inner Rescuer to soothe my pain, telling me I should disengage, walk back to my car, and leave my favorite island walk. Nothing on the outside had changed one iota!"

Sophia wrote in her journal what she did next:

*After taking a few steps, another inner voice said, "How about shifting your focus? How else might you experience this walk, the flowers, and gardens?" I stopped right there in the middle of the road and realized I had a choice. I did not have to Persecute myself—I could turn around, create a different experience. At that point I asked myself, "What experience do I want to create?" And I thought about my intention. I decided that, instead of comparing my garden to others, I wanted to truly experience the beauty I was seeing, without comparison or judgment. So, I turned around and kept walking. When I passed a trellis full of roses, I stopped and gently held one beautiful bloom in the palm of my hand, looking deeply at the wonder and magic of the petals, enjoying their colors and inhaling the fragrance. A moment of total awe and mystery.*

Sophia continued writing:

*It was so good to feel the difference from one moment to the next. This is what it means to update my human operating system and shift my focus from making something into a problem to asking myself what I really care about.*

Sophia was humbled by the power of this insight and its implications. She looked at the triangle she had drawn, then glanced up. People were coming and going from the cafe, ordering food, talking with friends. Life was going on pretty much as usual. But inside, she knew that this insight was bound to have a profound impact on her, and on her coaching clients as well.

Here was a way out of her long-held patterns of self-imposed victimhood, self-persecution, and self-rescuing—patterns that, only days before, had been invisible to her. Here, too, was a new framework to show RJ a way out of her castle prison, a way to lower the drawbridge and walk over that moat. She—and RJ, too—had the power to choose what thoughts to think and which roles to play at any moment, regardless of outside circumstances. What freedom!

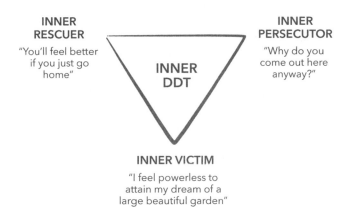

**INNER RESCUER**
"You'll feel better if you just go home"

**INNER PERSECUTOR**
"Why do you come out here anyway?"

**INNER DDT**

**INNER VICTIM**
"I feel powerless to attain my dream of a large beautiful garden"

*Diagram 3. The Inner DDT*

Sophia turned the page and started drawing The Empowerment Dynamic triangle—the positive alternative to the DDT. On this triangle the point was at the top. There she wrote *Inner Creator*, and beside that she wrote, *What do I want in this situation? What do I really care about right now?*

At the bottom left corner of the triangle, she wrote *Inner Challenger* and added, *I have courage to face uncomfortable situations. What is here for me to learn?*

At the bottom right corner of the triangle, Sophia wrote *Inner Coach*, along with the question, *How do I nourish and care for myself so that I'm able to effectively support others?*

In the middle of the triangle she wrote, *The Inner TED\* (\*The Empowerment Dynamic).*

Sophia pulled a sticky note from the inside flap of her journal. Thinking about the Inner TED\* prompted her to reflect more deeply on the shift from Rescuer to Coach in particular.

On the sticky note she wrote, *I've known that I am habitually a helper and lean toward the Rescuer role when relating to others. But how do I rescue myself when I have uncomfortable feelings? In this case I rescued myself from my own pain when I decided to stop walking and go back home. Think more about how the Inner Rescuer can show up in very sneaky ways.*

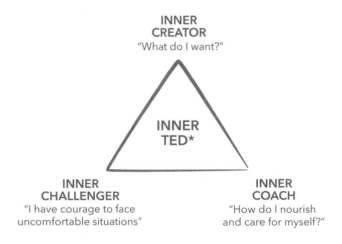

*Diagram 4. The Inner TED\**

She stuck the note to the top of the page, then noticed her server patiently standing nearby, holding her salad plate with its spring greens and warm sourdough roll on the side.

"Thank you, that looks wonderful," said Sophia. She put away her writing materials, still reflecting on the magnitude of her new insight.

After finishing lunch, Sophia picked up her journal again. Just then she felt the table gently vibrating. She picked up her phone and saw Gabe's face on their video app. He was calling!

"Hi, sweetie. How are you?"

"Doing well, Mom! Thanks for the mug—I like that quote. And I have plans for the birthday gift certificate! I've been needing a new fly-fishing rod for a while now. What are you doing today?"

"I just ate a nice salad at the café and was doing a little journaling."

"Your favorite spot," said Gabe.

"Yes. One of them, anyway!"

Her server appeared with the check. "Hey, Gabe, hold on for just a sec while I pay the bill," said Sophia. She counted out enough cash for the bill and a tip, and then picked up her bag and headed outside.

Outside the café, she sat down on a bench to enjoy a video chat with her son. They talked easily. Gabe and she always had plenty to say to each other. She knew from sharing with other parents of adult children that this wasn't always the case. In this moment, talking with her grown son on a beautiful afternoon after a nice lunch, Sophia felt lucky and grateful.

"How're you doing, Mom?"

"You know, I had quite a revelation on my walk last Sunday," said Sophia.

She shared how almost giving up her walk had inspired a realization of the shift from the Inner DDT to the Inner TED* roles. Gabe was a young boy when Sophia had first discovered those frameworks. Mom and son had learned in tandem about the DDT and TED* roles, often vying with each other to point out Victims, Persecutors, and Rescuers in the shows they watched together, and congratulating the characters inhabiting the TED* roles: "Way to go, Coach!" or "Go, Challenger!"

"That's really a new take on the triangles. I can use that," said Gabe. "I mean, I've known about the DDT for years, right? But I never thought about it as a map for my own thinking process. That's so cool."

He paused. "Actually, it reminds me of something that happened a few years ago, kind of similar to what happened for you on your walk."

"Really! Is this something you've told me about before?"

"Well, sort of. But not exactly." Sophia knew he was gauging how much he wanted to say. She wondered if Gabe was about to tell her about some way she had failed as his mother.

Gabe jumped in: "It was pretty soon after I moved to Colorado. It was great at first, but then, after a while I ran out of money. I didn't want to tell you about it because I knew you'd worry. But actually . . . there was a while when I was couch surfing at a couple of friends' apartments. And there were a few times I wasn't sure where my next meal was going to come from."

"Oh gosh," said Sophia, wincing.

"Anyway, one day I ended up busing tables at the ski lodge deli in exchange for a sandwich and a day ski pass," said Gabe. "I jumped on a lift chair to go to the top of the gnarliest ski run I'd been excited to try. There was one other guy on the chair, and it was a long ride up, so we talked a little. When he asked me what I did for a living, I was too embarrassed to say I didn't work . . . other than waiting tables in exchange for sandwiches and lift tickets. But I did say I was teaching myself digital design and that I was hoping to do websites for friends. So then, this guy said his company needed help with their website. When we jumped off the lift, he handed me his card and said to call him. I thought, 'Who carries business cards around in their ski pants?!' It was pretty amazing. And then we both headed off to ski."

"You must have felt so relieved," said Sophia, feeling relieved herself.

"Well, that's just it. What happened next is where I think my Inner DDT, as you're calling it, kind of took over. I think the Inner Persecutor voice started telling me stuff like, 'You don't even have a college degree! You aren't good enough at web design to work on some company's website!' The whole thing felt way too risky." Gabe got quiet for a moment.

"And then, I think my Inner Victim piled on the drama and made me feel powerless to get over my fear of talking to a company president. And then, let's see . . . my Inner *Rescuer* told me to just go have a good time, ski, and hang out with my friends. Above all, avoid calling the company president and the embarrassment that he'd find out I didn't know what I was doing."

There was a long pause. Sophia said, "Gabe, thank you for telling me all this . . . and for your willingness to be so vulnerable with your mom."

Gabe laughed, "Well, now you know the terrible truth! That's how I met the president of the company that makes the skis and snowboards I love. I never told you how that happened. I only told you the good parts: about getting a job with a company I believe in.

I wanted you to think I had polished up my résumé and got hired by outsmarting a bunch of other applicants."

"I guess that's understandable," said Sophia. "But you do know, don't you, that you can always tell me if you need my help?"

"Oh, I know that. I was a young dude then, out to prove I could make it on my own in the big, bad world." He grinned.

Sophia laughed and thought how, so far at least, the big bad world had been pretty kind to Gabe.

"Well, I love how you mapped your Inner DDT so quickly just now. But *then* what happened, because . . . you do work there now. So how did you transform your inner drama?"

"I have to hand you some credit, Mom. Because I grew up with those TED* roles, right? You'd always tell me, 'Gabe what do you care about? What do you want to create?'" He chuckled.

"For several days after I met the president of the company on the ski lift, I kept asking myself those same questions. I was afraid I wasn't good enough— that Inner Persecutor! But I could almost hear you saying how we have to muster the courage to challenge ourselves, to go after what we care about. Not what other people tell me I *should* care about, but what *I* really want. And that was why I moved to Colorado in the first place. I wanted to be close to the mountains and be able to ski, fish, and hike."

Sophia could see Gabe smiling broadly. He clearly appreciated this opportunity to come clean.

"Anyway, I had a long conversation with myself. I asked myself if I really cared about digital design or not. I decided yes, I cared enough to take at least one baby step. And that I didn't have to have it all figured out. So I called the number on his card.

"It was just one meeting, one conversation, but he was the president of my favorite skis and boards outfit, so at the time that was still a scary thought. I was half sure I was going to blow it."

Gabe continued, "I owe you one, Mom. You challenged me to focus on what I care about and then, if I really do care about something, to have the courage to keep growing. And to accept the responsibility to take one baby step at a time. You always say, 'The Creator essence wants to learn and grow—and that's our job as human beings.' Right?"

"Thanks, Gabe," said Sophia. She couldn't deny she felt pleased. "But I can claim only partial credit. I'm proud of that younger Gabe. You obviously dug deep into what you cared about, and your courage poured out from there. Because now here you are, doing the digital design for your company, having earned your community college degree. Pretty impressive."

"Thanks, Mom. But talking about it now, I can see how that whole deal changed the way I look at new experiences, or even just uncomfortable ones.

"If I didn't have the TED* roles to help me think it through, I might have missed out on a great job. But even back then, I didn't push away the fear of talking to the president. It felt weird at first, but once I arrived at their office, it didn't seem that scary anymore. After just that one meeting, he asked me to come aboard on a part-time basis to see how I would do. And obviously, it worked out. But the life lesson was, I can welcome any fear that may come with moving toward what I care about. That fear and anxiety wouldn't be there unless I cared about something.

"Isn't that what you've always said? That if I can embrace my fear, I'll have a whole different relationship with it?" Gabe flashed a big smile.

Sophia beamed. "How did you get so wise, young man?" They laughed.

"From you, Mom. Definitely," said Gabe. Then quickly he added, "Hey, I need to get back to work. Thanks for the talk and for my awesome birthday present. Can't wait to buy my new fly rod and try it out. And I've already had coffee in my new mug. Love you!"

Sophia held the phone a moment, staring at the red icon that signaled the end of their call. She took in the love she felt for Gabe. After a few deep breaths she brought herself back to the moment.

She looked at the time on her phone. "Time to get back, but there's really not a big rush," thought Sophia. She could take a couple of minutes to finish her journal entry.

She wrote, *Tara asked me to accept and nourish all the different parts of myself. If I resist doing that, she says the fearful parts will grow stronger and gain even more power and authority over me than they have now. Awakening my inner observer, facing those fearful parts, and listening to their voices will get me out of the grip of the DDT and into self-empowerment.*

Sophia paused and looked over what she had written, then added, *Honoring my ongoing struggles, inside and out, is the doorway to freedom and choice.*

# 9

## The Empowerment Dynamic

Sophia completed a client coaching call just in time to grab her bag and a travel mug of tea before driving downtown for an in-person session with RJ. It had been two weeks since their last video session, and she was happy that they had managed to schedule a longer session at RJ's office.

Sophia knew RJ was at a crossroads. Was she willing to do the heavy lifting to look within? It would mean facing the patterns of thought and behavior that had kept RJ trapped in her self-imposed castle. It wouldn't be easy.

She wondered if her client would commit to a longer-term coaching contract. "That will require her asking for support and encouragement to go beyond who she *thinks* she should be, to move toward who she really is," thought Sophia. After fifteen years of leadership coaching, she had learned that people change when they are ready, and not a minute before. What happened next would be up to RJ.

Maria greeted Sophia warmly, encouraging her to help herself to tea or coffee. Sophia was filling her mug with hot water to refresh her tea when RJ opened her office door. She looked genuinely happy to see Sophia as she motioned for her to come in. Above RJ's desk was the colorful new framed print.

"RJ, I like your new art even better in person," she said.

"Thanks, Sophia. I'm liking it, too, and I get nice comments from the staff. Most people think the bright colors are a bit out of character for me," said RJ, pointing. "I've been all business for so many years, I guess people are surprised I would take the time to shop for something like this."

"Well, what really counts is that you like it," said Sophia, taking a seat.

"I'm happy to be here in person and that we could schedule more time for today. It will allow for a deeper dialogue about the DDT and The Empowerment Dynamic roles and how they can help you understand what is happening within yourself at any given moment."

RJ jumped right in. "Since we talked about the DDT last time, I used my Notes app to record a few things, and I *do* see the DDT everywhere! Every commercial is about how victimized people feel about this or that—from bad plumbing to bad hair—and how the advertised product promises to rescue them. I hear it in conversations around the office, too. And the news cycle is full of the DDT, with every politician saying why they're the right one to rescue the country and save the day."

Sophia nodded, appreciating her client's new awareness.

RJ picked up her phone and tapped on it. "And here's a drama scenario I made some notes on." She read aloud: "Went to my sister's house for dinner."

RJ glanced up at Sophia. "Okay, William is my nephew," she explained, and continued: "William was persecuting his little sister, Emma, teasing her. Then their dad scolds William while hugging and rescuing Emma. William starts crying. So then my sister rescues him— she hugs William and says, 'Shh, I'll fix your favorite dessert tonight. That will make you feel better.'"

RJ set down her phone. "It was amazing, Sophia, how fast all that happened. I just stood back and observed. I realized how fast the roles change and how everyone races around the DDT, keeping the drama going!"

"Really nice job on observing and recording that family drama scene," said Sophia. "The DDT does seem to be the universal way we humans deal with uncomfortable feelings. And the more we learn about these roles, the more clearly we start to see our habits and how we relate to the world."

"I want to learn more about the other triangle!" RJ said, her voice rising with excitement. "How do I get out of this Dreaded Drama Triangle?"

"That's where we're going next," said Sophia. She reached into her bag, took out a sheet depicting the two triangles, and handed it to her. "You can keep this handout, RJ." She pulled out her pen to use as a pointer.

"Before we go on," Sophia began, "I want to make an important point that we covered briefly in our last session. When people first learn about these DDT roles, sometimes they overidentify with them and speak as though they *are* one particular role. They may say, 'Yes, I'm a Victim,' or 'I am a Rescuer'—"

RJ interjected, "Are you talking about before, when I said, 'I am a Persecutor?'"

"Yes," said Sophia. "I noticed last time that you—"

"I *don't like* that I am a Persecutor," blurted RJ. "Now that I see the DDT everywhere, the role I really detest is the Persecutor. And now I realize I *am* one!" she declared, clearly exasperated.

RJ leaned over the desk and looked closely at the DDT triangle on the handout. When she looked up again, her gaze was soft. "When I think about being a Persecutor, I just feel stuck."

Sophia was surprised at how quickly the session had become deeply personal for RJ. It was clear she had given a lot of thought to the DDT. But now she was identifying with the Persecutor role and using it to criticize herself.

Sophia felt empathy for RJ on this point. When she had first learned about the DDT she too had felt trapped initially, doomed to go racing from one reactive role to another. "Becoming more self-aware is essential to personal growth," she thought to herself, "but when we're facing the painful aspects of increased awareness, I've learned that is a time for self-compassion."

Only the Sunday before, on her favorite walk, Sophia had experienced how her Inner DDT could deliver mean-spirited messages. It had been a breakthrough in awareness for her to realize how she could use the DDT roles to examine her internal dialogue to see more clearly what she didn't want, as well as what she did want.

Sophia began slowly. "I hear you loud and clear. The Persecutor role is not who you want to be. That is wonderful, RJ."

"Wonderful?!" RJ retorted. "How can it be wonderful when I see how stuck I am? How, exactly, is that wonderful?"

Sophia took a deep breath, understanding the gravity of the moment. She wanted RJ to reap some progress from this new level of self-knowledge.

"The first step in changing and becoming the person you want to be," said Sophia, "is to embrace and acknowledge the parts of you that you don't like. It may seem counterintuitive, but it's true. When you honor and accept that part of you that sometimes plays the Persecutor role, you're beginning the journey toward nourishing the person you *really* are, down deep—your best self."

She continued, "The DDT roles are not meant to be used as mean names we call ourselves. They are ways of looking at how we are relating in a given moment. That means sometimes we have a Victim attitude, sometimes we become domineering like the Persecutor, and yes, sometimes we want to be accommodating like the Rescuer, to please others. There's nothing wrong with any of those parts of ourselves. In fact, they are all useful at various times, in certain situations. And once you can see your patterns revealed as the DDT roles, you have more awareness and can make more informed choices. But these are only *roles* you sometimes play; they are not who you are." Sophia paused.

RJ sat back in her chair with a long, deep sigh. Her frown softened, then her shoulders relaxed just a bit. Sophia thought she detected the beginnings of a smile.

Sophia said, "RJ, who you are, as a magnificent human being, is far more than the sum of the DDT roles. These roles are simply behavior strategies for managing your discomfort. When you can begin to observe those reactive roles as you are acting them out, you stand at a choice point. You can ask yourself, 'Do I want to stay in this DDT role right now, or do I want to shift toward what I want?'"

"Okay, Sophia," said RJ. "Message delivered. I'm starting to get your point. The DDT is a tool to understand what's happening. But how about we keep going with this—I need some tips so that when I do notice I'm stuck in the DDT, I can get *out* of those roles. Okay?"

Sophia smiled. "That's exactly it. We want to weaken the grip the DDT roles have on us. We do that by putting our attention on what we want. Can you think of an example this week when you may have felt stuck in the DDT, then shifted to what you wanted?"

RJ frowned slightly. "Well, since we talked last time, I've noticed how, when I focus on a problem and get really frustrated, my go-to role, as you call it, is to try to control the situation. I start taking charge of everything. I'm sure others see that as me persecuting them.

"That happened just this morning, in fact. A potential client was sitting out in the waiting room; they were interested in building a home in our new development and wanted to see the plan. But as I went out to meet them, Maria handed me the wrong drawings. When I noticed I had an outdated set of prints, I got really frustrated. I could tell I was starting to get angry. But this time, Sophia—you would have been proud of me—I asked myself, 'What am I focusing on?' I realized I was focusing on my need to look highly organized, especially in front of clients. And once I saw that, I also saw an easy solution.

"I excused myself and asked Maria to bring the latest drawings so my client could see the most up-to-date plan. When she handed me the correct prints, she apologized profusely. I said, 'It's okay, Maria. No harm, no foul.' As I walked back to my office, the whole episode actually seemed pretty minor. I don't know what shifted, but my frustration just kind of melted, and I was able to go back to the meeting minus the frustration."

"In the past I would've gotten so upset at Maria that I would have stopped focusing on my client's needs. I would have fumed about it all during the appointment, and then afterwards I probably would have yelled at Maria for making me look bad."

Sophia felt elated. "Do you see how much progress that is, RJ? For you to 'catch and correct' right in the moment? That's a big change!"

"Ha. 'Catch and correct,'" said RJ. "I like that. I'm going to remember that one." She made a note on her yellow pad. "I should plaster that across my forehead," she chuckled.

Sophia laughed, too. "Yes, that might be a helpful reminder for all of us!"

Sophia asked, "Do you remember the FISBE model we looked at, and how our problem-focused human operating system works? When we focus on problems we don't like, negative and uncomfortable feelings pop up in response to that focus. Then, we humans react to our *feelings* about the problem; we're not actually trying to solve the problem at all."

RJ jumped in. "I do remember the FISBE and how I fool myself—that I think I am just solving the problem, when really it's my *anxious feeling* about the problem that's got my attention."

"Good summary!" Sophia commented. What I'm hearing in your example with Maria is that you allowed yourself to feel your feelings without allowing them to overwhelm you. And, if I heard you correctly, your first thought was, 'I need to look highly organized to this client.' Is that correct?"

"Yes, something like that," said RJ. "But also, I suddenly realized that my client had no way of knowing whether I had the right drawings or not. That was when I decided to let go and just ask Maria to bring the updated prints. I'm so glad I didn't create a big drama the way I usually do." She grimaced.

"Nice job, RJ," said Sophia. "So, that example shows you're already learning to escape the grip of the DDT by asking yourself some key questions, starting with 'What do I want?' Another way to ask it is, 'What do I care about in this situation?' What I heard you say is that you cared more about focusing on your client's needs than you cared about being right or making Maria wrong."

RJ leaned forward. "I didn't realize that was what I asked myself, but now that you word it that way, that *is* what I asked. I shifted my focus to what I wanted— to simply have the right prints so I could discuss them with my client. Blaming Maria became irrelevant. It was so much easier!"

"It is easier, yes," agreed Sophia, "if you're willing to ask yourself what you want and then take responsibility for creating it. We call that the shift from Victim to Creator. You stopped being a Victim to your own reactive habits and became a Creator of what you wanted—to be of service to your clients." Sophia pointed her pen at the very top of the TED* triangle, labeled *Creator*. "It really is that simple, but it's not always easy."

Sophia paused to let the comparison sink in. "The Creator is the positive alternative to the Victim role in the DDT. The Creator plays the central role in the TED* triangle."

"TED*?" asked RJ, glancing at the diagram. "That's the name of the second triangle? You call it *TED*\*?"

"Yes, it stands for *The Empowerment Dynamic*. I learned it from a wise and wonderful older gentleman whose name happens to also be Ted. But he swears he didn't name it after himself."

Sophia smiled. "Pretty cool, huh?"

"Interesting," said RJ.

Sophia continued, "When we're inhabiting the Victim role, we feel powerless over whatever is going on. We think life is something that is happening *to* us. In that role, we've given up our power to outside circumstances or other people, convinced that we can't get what we want in life. So, we whine and complain about all the things going on 'out there.'

"The uniqueness of the Victim role," said Sophia, "is that we look for someone, or something, to rescue us and fix the situation. Victim language sounds like this: 'I can't, I don't know how, It isn't fair, or There's not enough.'"

"But Sophia," RJ objected, "I don't say those things. I do hear them from other people, though."

Sophia paused for a moment. "I'm curious, RJ, when your dad died suddenly and you inherited your role as CEO of this company, do you remember what you said to yourself? I appreciate that it was a long time ago, but just think back to whatever you remember. Take your time, okay?"

RJ looked up at the ceiling, then off to one side, her chin resting in her hand. At last she said, "I actually do remember. I did tell myself, 'This isn't fair. This is ruining my life.' And I thought, 'Why me?'" She sank back in her chair. "So, I guess I did say those things, back then at least."

Sophia empathized. "That must have been a very hard time for you, RJ. And yet, you obviously learned to take charge. What did you do to meet all that responsibility?"

"Looking back now, it makes more sense. I did say 'Poor me' and 'I don't know how.' But I had to cover up all the insecurity I felt, so the first thing I did was fire a few people that were underperforming, just to let everyone know I was boss."

RJ suddenly looked sad. "Is that how I became a Persecutor? I felt like a Victim, being hurled into this job without enough preparation. But the *last* thing I wanted was to be a Victim, so I started blindly trying to control everyone and everything."

Sophia allowed the silence to rest and expand, curious as to how RJ was making sense of her new insights. RJ straightened in her chair and asked, "Why should I care about seeing my DDT roles, though? I mean, why does this even *matter*?"

"Do *you* have a sense of why it matters?" Sophia asked, interested to hear where RJ was going with this confrontation. But then RJ jumped in.

"I guess the point is, if I can see how I get stuck in the DDT roles, then hopefully I can learn to spend less time on the Drama Triangle—less unproductive time—reacting to what I don't want."

"Exactly, RJ. You can't change a habit until you can see it. Noticing and naming your DDT roles helps you see how you may have unconsciously overused parts of yourself, and how continuing to do that can cause you anxiety and lead you to sabotage your best self."

Sophia continued, "Once you see your DDT habits, you have a choice. You no longer have to be a Victim to what you thought or felt in the past. You can choose to be a Creator of your own life. When you embrace your Creator role, RJ, you accept who you are as a human being—your strengths and all the best parts of you."

Sophia paused for a moment. RJ was gazing intently at the two triangles on the handout.

"When you shared your story about Maria giving you the wrong drawings," said Sophia, "you used Creator language. When you talked about shifting your focus to what you cared about—focusing on your client's needs—you described the shift from the Victim role to the Creator role.

"That Creator essence in us asks powerful questions such as 'What do I want? What do I care about?'

"The Creator also asks, 'What is mine to do? What is it my responsibility to create? What is it I want in this moment? How do I choose to respond to what's happening?' There's a big difference between Victim language and the Creator language."

"I can see how those are different sets of questions," RJ mused. She seemed to be grasping the magnitude of the shift from victimhood to empowerment.

Sophia continued, "The shift from Victim to Creator means taking responsibility for all your choices and actions. It means owning your power to choose, rather than giving your power away to circumstances and waiting for someone or something to rescue you."

RJ nodded firmly. "But I also know it is easier said than done."

"Yes," Sophia admitted. "I agree with you there. And guess what, you've already shared that you know how to make that shift. In your story about the architectural drawings, you shifted from feeling victimized by not having the correct prints . . . to focusing on what you wanted on behalf of your clients."

RJ pushed her chair back from her desk. "Thanks, Sophia, for that feedback. But that was just one time. That doesn't mean I know how to do this!"

Sophia remained firm. "That's certainly possible. At the same time, I want to support you in recognizing that, while it may not always be easy, you actually *do know* how to make the shift from Victim to Creator."

She went on, "Most of us make this positive shift sometimes. But because the DDT is so familiar, and because our default human operating system tends to focus on problems and what we don't like, it is easy to spend more time stuck in the DDT than being our natural selves as Creators. So, it's very important to acknowledge and celebrate the times when you *don't* get stuck in the DDT—when you're living from your Creator essence. That is the foundational shift from DDT to TED*."

Sophia paused to see if RJ wanted to add anything. When she didn't, Sophia continued.

"What do you say, RJ? Are you okay with moving on to consider the shift from Persecutor to Challenger now?" asked Sophia.

"Okay. Keep going," agreed RJ matter-of-factly, leaning forward to get a better look at the handout.

Sophia used her pen to point to the Challenger role at the lower left corner of the TED* triangle. "The Challenger is the positive alternative to the Persecutor role. The Challenger is the truth teller in us. It is the part of us that sees reality as it is, and summons the will and the courage to step up in order to learn and grow. Creating is not always easy, so the Creator needs its partner, the Challenger, to call forth the commitment and energy to keep moving forward, even when things look bleak or impossible.

"The Challenger's energy is bold and strong as well as clear and direct. The role of the Challenger is to build up, to grow and learn without judgment or blame."

"Like I did when I took charge of the company after my dad died?" RJ interjected.

"Great question," said Sophia. "Hearing your story, I would say that you certainly took charge. Let me ask you, RJ: In that example, what was your intention in taking charge?"

"It was very clear," said RJ proudly. "My intention was to not fail, so people wouldn't think I didn't know what I was doing. I didn't want to look bad. People were already worried that RJ Construction wouldn't be solid without my dad at the helm. If I had let my leadership team and employees see me sweat, it would have been a PR nightmare."

RJ stopped short. "Oh geez," she said, "I know what you are going to ask me next. You're going to ask me what was I focusing on, right? Don't ask me. I was focused on all the things I didn't want to happen. I was focusing on *myself*, on not looking bad. Ugh. That isn't exactly what you described as a Challenger, is it? I am not liking this revelation at all."

"Thank you for your honesty and vulnerability, RJ," Sophia said. "When we get stuck in the Persecutor role, our intention usually *is* to look good, to win, and to be right. That means finding a scapegoat and putting others down." Sophia took a breath and slowed the pace. RJ's head was bent and she stared at the desktop as though examining the wood grain.

"On the other hand," Sophia continued brightly, "when we're in the role of a Challenger, our intention is to grow—to be continuously learning while supporting others as well. We urge ourselves on to be our best selves, and we support others to be at their best, too.

"Now, what would you say Persecutor language sounds like, RJ?"

"That's easy. I've said those things plenty of times: 'You're doing it wrong. You should have listened to me. I knew I was right. Do it this way, not'—"

Sophia raised her hand with a chuckle. "Okay, RJ. It's obvious you have a firm grasp of the Persecutor role! Those are great examples of what we say, or think, when we're stuck in that role."

RJ smiled. "I could have given you a lot more."

"I don't doubt that," said Sophia, softening. "It's a role you've associated with your survival as a leader, and you've been resorting to it for a long while now. But when this energy is overused and becomes the only way you know to respond to life's challenges, then it becomes a limitation. The Challenger's purpose and intention is very different from the Persecutor's.

"One way to understand the Challenger role is to think of someone in your life who encouraged you. You may have felt they were being really tough on you. It might have been a teacher, a grandparent, or a sports coach. Can you think of someone who challenged you . . . in a way that ultimately helped you, even if their doing so was a little uncomfortable at the time?"

RJ thought for a moment. "The first person who comes to mind is my urban economics professor in college. He was tough, for sure. He pulled me aside after class one day and said I was not performing like he knew I could. He told me, 'I expect more of you and I know you can do it if you apply yourself.' I hated hearing that! At first, I guess I saw him as a Persecutor, although I didn't have that language at the time. But at some point, I saw that he believed in me and just wanted me to excel. The way you're explaining this role of Challenger—that's what he was doing. I managed an A- in his class, mainly because he challenged me."

"Great example of someone who challenged you to be your best and step up," said Sophia. "It sounds like his intention was clear—to encourage you to grow and learn."

"Yes, definitely," agreed RJ. "His intention was not to put me down or belittle me, even though I took it that way at first. But tell me something: Why do you call the Challenger role the truth teller?"

Sophia smiled. "What's your guess?"

After a pause, RJ said, "Well, I guess we need a tough partner—someone who will hold us accountable and won't hesitate to talk about the elephant in the room. If we don't tell the truth to ourselves and others, then who will? Is that it?" RJ asked, looking pleased with herself.

"I've never heard it explained in just that way before, RJ, but frankly, that is one of the most insightful descriptions I've heard. Nice job," Sophia said, and took a brief moment to pause before she spoke again.

"In summary, an important question we ask ourselves in order to shift from Victim to Creator is, 'What do I, or we, want?' and the question that supports the shift from Persecutor to Challenger is, 'What is my intention?'"

"Thanks for that recap, Sophia. I've realized in our conversation today if I notice a DDT role in action, I also have to remember not to beat myself up about it, so I can choose to shift to the empowering role, right?"

"You've got it! Let's take a break now, and then we can consider the shift from Rescuer to Coach. This work requires a lot of emotional energy, so it is good to pause and refresh ourselves," Sophia said. "How about ten minutes and we start again?"

"Okay. Sounds good," RJ said as she got up from her chair and moved toward the door.

# 10

## From Rescuer to Coach

After a brief walk around the building and a few nibbles from her snack bag, Sophia returned to the CEO's office and sat down to wait for RJ. In the sudden quiet, Sophia became increasingly aware of her thoughts. They began with a trickle that quickly turned into a geyser. Her Inner Persecutor was up to its old tricks again.

"You're acting like you're perfect," the critical voice chided, "giving RJ the impression that you never get stuck in the DDT yourself, which you know you do! The way you're teaching this material, she must think you're some kind of saint!"

Then a new thought arose, and Sophia felt her inner drama moment recede: "The last thing I want to do is give RJ the idea that I have all this stuff all figured out—that I never go reactive in my own life. On the contrary, now that I'm aware of the DDT I catch it showing up more often than ever. The main difference is that now I can choose whether to stay stuck, or nourish my best self to step forward."

RJ walked in and sat down. "Ready?"

"Ready." Sophia pulled herself back to the moment and reminded herself to continue breathing fully and remain present. "Okay, RJ. How did it feel to take a break?"

"How did that feel?" RJ replied with a puzzled look. "It felt good to walk around and get some fresh air for a few minutes, but I had the strong urge to go back to work. I don't have time for breaks, typically. In fact, I should be working right now." She chuckled half-heartedly, then added, "Just kidding, I think."

Hearing this report from RJ's Inner Persecutor, Sophia felt an instant kinship with RJ. The message might be different, but the self-criticism was much the same.

"I feel more refreshed, too. Are you ready to move on to the third DDT-to-TED* shift—from the Rescuer role to the Coach role?" Sophia said. "I know this one pretty well. The Rescuer role is how I often enter the DDT myself, so I have a lot of experience with the complexity of this particular role."

"Complexity? How is it complex?" asked RJ. "I remember you saying the Rescuer acts like the hero, the helper. That sounds straightforward to me."

"It's true, the Rescuer can be described as the helper or the pleaser," said Sophia. "Personally, though, I prefer the phrase *pain reliever*. The Rescuer shows up when we don't like the emotions that arise in the moment. The Rescuer labels upsetting emotions as a problem, then immediately wants to relieve the pain of those anxious feelings, trying to fix whatever it sees as being 'wrong.'"

Sophia continued, "One of the complexities in transforming the Rescuer role is the high value that our society and most cultures place on being a helper.

When compared to the other two DDT roles of Victim or Persecutor, the Rescuer looks pretty good.

"Few people want to admit when they're playing the Victim role. Even more say that they detest the Persecutor role outright. I think you also used the word *detest* when speaking about the Persecutor role. Am I remembering that correctly?"

"That's right. And I *do* detest it," affirmed RJ. "But I feel a *little* better about it now that I understand how I got stuck in that role in the first place."

"Most people say they don't mind defaulting to the Rescuer because it sounds like something a 'nice' person does," Sophia said. "That's why making the shift out of the Rescuer role can get a bit complex. It's important to try to see the shadow side of the Rescuer."

"I'm not sure what you mean by the 'shadow side.'" RJ frowned slightly.

"The word *shadow* in this context is a psychological term," said Sophia. "It describes any part of ourselves that we don't want to see, or more precisely, a side of ourselves we *can't* see. If we repress this part and push it down, or disown it, it goes unconscious. Hence its name. It hides in the shadows. The trouble is, if we are not aware of its power, the shadow side of us can operate on its own. It may assume control over much of our thinking and behavior."

Sophia pointed to the DDT triangle on the handout. "Remember, when we're in the Victim role we think or say, 'Poor me' or 'Why me?' The Victim sees the Persecutor as the problem. The Persecutor, for its part, is committed to never being a Victim, so it uses control and blame to stay one up—"

RJ broke in. "Like I was committed to not being a Victim when Dad died . . . so I resorted to the Persecutor role. Right?"

"Sounds like that really makes sense to you," said Sophia.

"Now that I see it, I can't possibly *not* see it! But let's get back to the Rescuer," RJ said. "Are you saying that the Rescuer's need to save the day is a response to something unconscious? Just like I was unconscious of not wanting to be a Victim?"

"That's it exactly," said Sophia. "You're a quick learner, RJ. Once the Victim-Persecutor dynamic gets going, it can trigger the Rescuer to solve the tension between those other two roles."

RJ looked down and sighed. "I can totally see how that happens."

"It's something we all do some of the time," Sophia said. "When we get stuck in this way of relating, the Rescuer language is distinct and easy to spot. We say things like 'Let me help,' or 'I can fix this,' or 'Don't worry, I'll take care of it.'

"But it doesn't always stop there. If the Rescuer's pleasing and helping behavior turns obsessive, it actually *needs* Victims or situations to fix. A person who gets deeply stuck in the Rescuer role becomes unconscious about how much their worthiness depends on making others happy. And that's an exhausting way to go through life.

"When understanding human behavior, RJ, there are no absolutely fixed rules. But we can apply frameworks like the DDT to become more self-aware and to help us reflect on our unique situation. For example, I was told as a little girl to always smile and 'be nice,' so it felt natural to me to take on the Rescuer role. Of course, there's nothing innately wrong with that. Helpful, kind people are hugely important contributors to the greater good. At the same time, it's important to be aware of our motivation and what needs we are trying to fulfill . . . *whatever* we're doing."

Sophia continued, "There's a metaphor I use to imagine what it's like when I'm in the Rescuer role. I become like a lighthouse, scanning the environment for people or situations that need my help, convincing myself that others need my guiding light for their very survival. But when I'm operating from this belief, it can act as a justification to overstep others' boundaries. I'm viewing the other person as incapable of navigating the rough waters of life and taking responsibility for themselves."

As she described the metaphor to RJ, Sophia recalled the exhaustion she had often felt over the years. Standing strong in support of others, trying her best to be helpful, only to experience later that, in the process of all that rescuing, her own light had grown dim.

"Until I began studying the DDT," added Sophia, "I had no idea how much harm one could do when unconsciously moving through life in the Rescuer role."

"Not sure I follow you, Sophia. What harm can a Rescuer do?" RJ looked incredulous.

"This may be a good moment to pause, RJ. Think about the Rescuer role and how it might potentially have a negative impact on others," Sophia said.

RJ responded. "Keep going. I'm thinking about that. I may even have an example to share, but I'm not entirely sure how it makes sense that someone being helpful could cause harm."

"It's like this," Sophia said. "Even when I do something to be helpful to others, if what I'm doing is *their* responsibility, I'm disempowering them. In the Rescuer role, I'm usually doing that unwittingly, of course. But it still robs them of their dignity, removing their chance to make their own decisions and to learn and grow in their own way. We actually reinforce their sense of victimhood. That's the harm we can do, all in the name of being a helper."

Sophia continued, "Ultimately an out-of-control Rescuer ends up needing someone with a Victim mentality to feed their need to be helpful. When we're stuck in the Rescuer role, we see others mainly as Victims rather than as Creators. If we see someone's Creator essence, we may still offer help, but we respect their right to lead their own lives, even when they're struggling."

"Sophia, are you saying that the Rescuer actually seeks out situations where they can be a hero?"

"What's your impression, RJ?"

"Well," RJ said, a bit defensively, "I may not consciously *look* for those situations, but I do often encounter people who seem to be looking for my help like they can't do it for themselves."

Sophia remembered the sticky note she had put in her journal after writing about the Rescuer role at the café. "Defaulting to the Rescuer role for so long gave me a valuable chance to understand the complexity behind the simplicity of all the DDT roles," she thought to herself. "Today I'm grateful for that."

She continued, "Another epiphany I've had about these DDT roles, RJ, is how quickly we can switch from one role to another. Rescuers think they are helping, but often they put their nose into other people's business and then they are seen as unwelcome Persecutors. The Rescuer then feels like a Victim when they get criticized for overstepping. Everyone in the situation is then racing around the DDT!"

"I see that a lot," said RJ. "You know, I thought I was just a Persecutor, but actually, when I want people to appreciate me, that calls up the Rescuer in me. Something happened a few weeks ago where I definitely overstepped, and it caused a *lot* of drama." She rolled her eyes.

"Oh?" Sophia's eyebrows went up. "Please share if you'd like to."

"Sure," she said sheepishly. "I told my team that I wanted to continue our tradition of the company picnic," said RJ. "I asked for volunteers to plan the picnic and make all the arrangements. Then a few days later, I decided to surprise everyone by buying all the food. I had Maria order barbecue from a local caterer everyone likes.

"When I showed up at the picnic planning meeting, I was excited to report that the barbecue had been ordered and paid for by the company. I thought everyone would be grateful. Instead they all looked at me with . . . well, horror, actually. Finally, John spoke up and said, 'RJ, that's nice of you to pay for it, but we've already planned the food. It's going to be a potluck. Everyone wanted to share their favorite dish.'

"It was so awkward, Sophia. I didn't know what to say. It hadn't even occurred to me to ask what they wanted. It's a perfect example of how I *say* I want employee involvement, but then I take over." RJ looked embarrassed and a little relieved.

"Thank you for sharing that, RJ. It must have been difficult to sit through the rest of that meeting realizing you asked them to plan the picnic but then hadn't trusted them to take charge. I'm curious about how you see yourself as a Rescuer in that story."

"Well. I wanted to be helpful by buying the food," said RJ. "Isn't that what you said is behind the Rescuing role? Being overly helpful when it isn't my responsibility?"

"Okay. If I understand, then," reflected Sophia, "you were trying to please them by ordering the food so they didn't have to pay for it. Is that correct?"

"Yes," said RJ.

"What was your payoff for doing that?" asked Sophia.

"My *payoff*?" RJ asked incredulously. "You mean what did I want in return for buying the food? Hmm." RJ looked genuinely perplexed. She thought for a moment.

"I guess I do know what I wanted . . . but I hate to admit it." She winced.

Sophia was fairly sure she knew what RJ was about to say. But instead of jumping in with a guess, she took a relaxing breath. She knew there was value in maintaining a calm silence while RJ sat with her uncomfortable feelings. Sophia coached herself: "You don't need to rescue RJ from her discomfort with another question or comment. Just let the silence be."

RJ shifted in her chair. She leaned back and stretched her arms over her head for a moment, then squared her elbows on the desktop. She said, "I did it because I wanted them to like me. I hoped they would appreciate me for being a good boss."

Sophia knew it took courage for RJ to admit that to herself, and to share it. RJ just wanted her team to like her for being a good boss. She probably also wanted affirmation that she was a good person. That story wasn't really about her workers or the barbecue or the picnic—it was about her.

"Thanks for your honesty, RJ. You've accurately described the delusion of the Rescuer role," Sophia said. "The Rescuer thinks they are 'helping others,' but in reality, the bid to help is all about 'me' and the need to be loved and appreciated."

As a recovering Rescuer, Sophia knew how painful it could be to lift the veil of that delusion and see the self-interest underneath all that 'helping and giving and pleasing.' At the same time, she knew clearly that her pattern of rescuing was only a role—one she often fell into, yes, but certainly not her whole identity.

"I'm right there with you, RJ," said Sophia. "I know the pain and embarrassment of that realization. I can't tell you how many times I've overstepped the bounds of my responsibility, helping and fixing other people's problems when it wasn't mine to do. And why? Because I wanted to be liked, even loved, in return. That's a hard fact for us Rescuer types to face—that what is behind our helping behavior, our 'good deeds,' is the hope that we will earn love and appreciation in return."

RJ looked astonished. "I never realized that before, but it's so obvious now. I thought I was just trying to be helpful, but it was clear they all saw me in that moment as a Persecutor. I heard some whispers in the hall after that: 'There she goes again, putting her nose in where she doesn't belong.'"

"You described it well. That's how, when we get stuck in the Rescuer role, we inevitably end up in the Victim role. Because ultimately, those we are trying to fix often don't *want* our 'wonderful ideas.' They don't want our interference, so they push back, sometimes really hard. And then how do we feel?" Sophia held out her open hand as a cue for RJ to answer.

"Like Victims!" piped RJ.

"Yes! But once we see how the Rescuer pattern can disable others and add lots of fuel to the drama, we have a chance to transform it."

"Thank goodness!" said RJ.

Sophia continued, "Now, please don't misunderstand. Being supportive and helpful toward others is core to our humanity. It is an essential attribute for loving relationships. Becoming aware of our *motivation* for helping is the key.

"The positive alternative to the Rescuer role is the Coach," she went on. "And when I say *Coach*, I don't mean a professional coach like myself. All of us have a coach in us—the part of us that asks questions, that is curious. In the Coach role, rather than telling and fixing, we let go of our need to be a helpful hero, and instead get really curious about what's going on. And a reminder: When I say *curious*, it is the friendly curiosity that we talked about a few sessions ago, not the probing curiosity.

"A few minutes ago, you alluded to the key shift that signals the Coach role. Do you remember what you said?"

"Gosh, I'm not sure," said RJ. "My head is swimming with all this new information. What did I say?"

"You said that you hadn't asked the employees what they wanted. Coaching, as the alternative to rescuing, is about asking questions, getting curious about what others want and need. Instead of merely assuming you know what others need or want, a Coach leaves that power with the other person. So we don't just leap in and do for others what we *think* they need—we *ask* what they need. It may seem like a small shift in our motivation, but in practice, it's gigantic."

RJ looked away for a moment, then back at the handout. Sophia moved her pen to the lower right corner of the handout toward the TED* triangle and pointed to the name *Coach*.

"Beginning the shift from Rescuer to Coach is an inside-out process. What I mean by that is it begins when someone stuck in the Rescuer role focuses on their self-care and fulfilling their own needs. That's difficult for we Rescuer types who think our purpose in life, and even our value as a human being, depends on helping others. If we focus on caring for ourselves, we feel it's a 'guilty pleasure'—we think we're being selfish. At least that's what I experience when I'm stuck in the Rescuer role."

RJ leaned forward, studying the handout closely. "I didn't expect you to say that. I'm not following why the Rescuer needs to take care of themselves first. I don't get the connection."

Sophia continued, "The Rescuer believes their job is to support *others*, so if they take care of themselves, they feel as if they are failing at their job of taking care of others.

"But our Creator essence is innate to the human spirit," Sophia continued. "Once we recognize that for ourselves, I believe we have no choice but to accept that other people have the same Creator essence as well. That truth may set us free, but before it does, it rocks our boat!"

"I guess if I had seen the people on our company picnic planning committee as Creators, I would have trusted their capacity to lead on their own without my help. Is that what you're saying, Sophia?"

"How does that insight resonate for you as you say it, RJ?"

"Well, what I *think* I'm understanding is that if I had seen them as capable to plan the picnic, then I could have asked them what they wanted or needed from me in the way of support. Right?"

"Asking that question would leave the power with them, yes," agreed Sophia. "As a leader, you clearly provided a vision to have a company picnic. But then the key comes when you must let go and allow them to lead, reminding them you are there if they have questions or need your help. That's when the fun starts. You get to be really curious about how the picnic will turn out!

"To cultivate the ability to stay in the Coach role, we have to learn to enjoy not knowing how things are going to turn out. The Rescuer in us likes things to go as we plan so everyone is happy. But that bid to overly influence and direct a situation is the very reason why others often see the Rescuer as a Persecutor, trying to control a particular outcome."

"There's that word *control* again," said RJ, wincing.

"RJ, it may surprise you to hear this, but *all three* of the DDT roles are attempting to exert control—to avoid something you don't like or don't want. The roles themselves are behavior patterns . . . and all three are problem-focused, anxiety-driven, and reactive in nature, so they have a lot in common. In that sense, all three roles are the result of a 'Victim mentality.' That's the origin of the dance of drama!" Sophia said, waving her hand with a theatrical flourish.

"Geez. I hadn't realized all three DDT roles had that much in common, but I can see that now. I've learned a lot today," she said.

"The good news is," Sophia added, "once you can catch that drama just before it happens in real time, you have a way out of it. You can call on the TED* roles to liberate you from the DDT!"

Sophia waited to see if RJ had any other thoughts to add. Instead, she suddenly seemed to disengage. With a slight frown, she pushed away from the desk and leaned back in her chair. Then she let out a big sigh.

Noticing the shift in body language, Sophia asked, "How are you feeling right now, RJ?"

RJ paused a moment before responding. "Actually . . . I don't know. Just thinking, I guess. When Roger mentioned the idea of working with you, I had no idea it would be . . . that it would be so much about me." She glanced at Sophia.

Sophia wasn't surprised to hear RJ's hesitancy about engaging in the deep personal inquiry she knew was an integral part of the coaching process. Sophia checked in with herself and silently reflected: "Usually at this point I'm hoping my clients are ready to go deeper into transforming the personal habits that stand in their way. But I'm finally learning that coaching is always about the client—and what they are ready for! It feels good to let go of the wish for my clients to do what I think they 'should' do. It feels right to accept and love them as they are, without expecting them to be any different. Maybe I am finally and fully learning the shift from Rescuer to Coach!"

RJ broke in on her reverie. "Sophia, I'd really like to learn more about how to get off the Drama Triangle."

"Yes, that's the key, isn't it?" said Sophia. "I would say there are three basic steps. First step is noticing and weakening the grip the drama roles have on you. The second step is applying various tools to help with that. I call them TED* Tools, and we've talked about several of those: the Three Levels of Listening, Telling Three Stories, getting curious, catching and correcting. And you also practiced 'naming and noticing' your DDT roles. And all of the TED* Tools support the last step in breaking out of the Drama Triangle— strengthening the awareness and emergence of your Creator, Challenger, and Coach roles."

"That's very helpful, thinking of the process as three basic steps. You make it sound simple and I know they're not simple, but I can see the steps we covered," RJ said.

"We have covered a lot, and you have been very engaged and shared powerful insights. It is time to wrap up now. Do you have any additional questions before we go about what's next?"

RJ shook her head, then said, "No, I don't think so."

"There is just one more thing to consider, then, at this point," said Sophia. "Our coaching contract was for a few introductory sessions over these past two months. During that time, the desired outcomes you stated were to experience coaching and to sort through some of the issues you presented in our first session. You also asked that I share some of the information that Roger told you was so meaningful for him. Do you feel we have focused on those outcomes?"

RJ sat up straighter. "Yes, good summary. That is what we talked about at the beginning."

Sophia continued, "At this point, RJ, I suggest entering into a yearlong coaching contract tailored to the outcomes you want, in order to support you in becoming the leader you wish to be." She took out of her folder a one-page brief description of her coaching program, recommended calendar, and its fees, and slid it across the desk toward RJ.

"I'll leave this with you. Given what you've shared and the points we've covered, I recommend you take a little while to decide your next steps and readiness to continue with your personal learning journey. Before I leave today, we can schedule a check-in call if you like. How does that sound?"

RJ said she liked that idea. She told Sophia she had learned so much in the few coaching sessions that she wanted to consider where she stood regarding her business in general and her goals for her leadership team in particular.

Sophia continued, "Now is a good time for reflection and to begin integrating what you've learned. You have had some powerful new insights. It's up to you when, or whether, to enter into a longer coaching agreement. In any case, I want you to know I'll respect your choice."

"Thanks for that, Sophia. I'll take some time to think about it. I'll be in touch very soon."

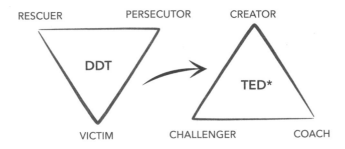

*Diagram 5. The Shift from DDT to TED\**

# 11

## The Inner Persecutor and the Unhelpful Helper

Sophia had been enjoying a relaxing morning. After breakfast she had gone out to the porch to give her potted flowers a good watering, reveling in the warm sunshine. Her next task was to write an email to Gabe. Over the weekend she had a sudden burst of energy and decided to clean what had been her son's old bedroom. She found several items in the closet and wanted to check in with him about what to do with his old clothes and gear, plus it was a welcome excuse to connect with him. Although her son had moved out of the house over five years earlier, Sophia kept his room pretty much as it was when he left. Gabe visited home more and more infrequently now, and Sophia was finally facing that it was time to clear out what was left of his things.

In her email, Sophia listed the stray items: Nike basketball shoes, two like-new sweatshirts, several flannel shirts, a baseball glove, a box of baseball cards, some posters, a video game player and half a dozen video games.

*Did you want me to ship only some or all of these to you in Colorado?* wrote Sophia. *Just let me know fairly soon while I'm still in the cleaning mood.* She chuckled as she finished the email with her usual *I love you* and a smiley face emoji.

Sophia still had a few minutes left before her check-in call with RJ, so she glanced at her to-do list for her upcoming mini-vacation to the beach. Sophia was eagerly planning what she would need to pack up tomorrow morning for her leisurely three-day weekend. For weeks she had looked forward to this time off. It hardly seemed possible that it was only a year since she last visited her favorite cottage on the beach. Most of all, she was excited to see her good friend and mentor, Tara. Sophia rummaged through her desk drawer to locate her earbuds, then snatched up two novels from the stack of books on her coffee table. She crossed those items off her list. Her groceries were already packed, including the chocolate chip cookies she had made the night before for a weekend treat.

Since they had met on Clear Beach fifteen years ago, Tara and Sophia had made it a point to create time to get together once a year. Their beach visits had become an essential way for Sophia to renew her energy and connect with Tara. Just thinking about walking up and down the speckled sand with the ocean breeze in her face gave Sophia the shivers! The weather report was sunny and her favorite cottage, now a rental, was reserved and awaiting her arrival. "It won't be long now," she thought. "I just need to stay focused on work for a few more hours and then I'm out of here!" She did a little half jig on her way to the kitchen, where she refreshed her tea, then headed to her office.

Sophia sat down at her desk to prepare for her call with RJ at the top of the hour. It had been two weeks since their last appointment at RJ's office. It had been a power-packed two-hour session, with Sophia sharing more TED* Tools to use in shifting from the DDT roles to the TED* roles—out of drama and into creatorship. They had agreed, at Sophia's suggestion, that RJ would take some time to think about the next step in her leadership journey.

At the close of that session, Sophia had recommended to RJ a yearlong leadership coaching program tailored to support RJ and address her vision for herself as well as the challenges she was facing as leader of RJ Construction. RJ had been intrigued with how to get off the Drama Triangle and seemed genuinely interested in learning more. The price of the program was reasonable, too, given the value RJ would receive, both personally and professionally. If RJ chose to keep learning, the program would put her in a strong position to lead the company for many years to come.

Sophia opened Zoom on her laptop and waited for RJ to arrive on the call. In a couple of minutes her client appeared onscreen, waving hello. "Hey Sophia, how are you?" Sophia waved back and said hello, then noticed her audio was still muted. Before she could unmute and say hello again, RJ jumped right in.

"It was good to take some time to think about the coaching program you mentioned. I read the information you gave me, and I've thought a lot about it," said RJ.

Then, without skipping a beat, she added, "The time just isn't right for me, Sophia. I'm going to pass."

Sophia thought to herself, "Boy, RJ really does get right to the point." Sophia straightened her posture, took a deep breath, and did her best to relax. She told herself to listen deeply in Levels Two and Three: "Listen for what is not being said, between RJ's words," she thought. "Listen for her energy and her feeling."

RJ continued, saying how many new clients had come in for the company in only the past two weeks, how suddenly it seemed that everyone wanted to build, and that there was just too much on her plate now to add another nice-to-have.

RJ said, "I really need to concentrate on the business right now. There's so much going on here at the office. The low interest rates have created a strong market for new homes. So, my focus needs to be on making sure our business runs smoothly. I am going to pass on that coaching program," she repeated.

Sophia said, "I understand, RJ." Before she could say more, RJ interrupted.

"I've learned so much from you already," she said, a bit breathlessly. "That summary flyer you gave me of The Empowerment Dynamic and the two triangles is on my desk, and I look at it a lot to think about what I am focusing on and what role I may be playing. I've enjoyed our sessions, but the time just isn't right for more. Let's stay in touch and maybe have lunch someday when things settle down."

Sophia had learned that when she was hit with a surprise, or when a client talked nonstop, it was best to take a few deep belly breaths, relax her shoulders, feel her feet on the ground, and stay centered. She did that now as she wished RJ well.

"I'd like to stay in touch, too, RJ. One way to do that, if you like, is to subscribe to my weekly blog about The Empowerment Dynamic. You could respond by email whenever a topic resonates with you," Sophia said.

"Of course," said RJ, clearly eager to end the call. "Please sign me up for your blog. That sounds like a good plan. Thanks again, Sophia. Take good care and be safe, you hear?" RJ cheerfully waved goodbye and within seconds Sophia was looking at her own face onscreen. RJ had signed off.

Sophia sat staring at the screen for a moment as her mind wandered.

"Well, looks like I called that one wrong," she thought. "I was pretty confident that RJ appreciated her new insights. I guess I misread her cues." She gazed out the window. Bees hovered near the flowers that dripped from the hanging planter.

"Or maybe my strong need to be of service and fix the world's problems stopped me from accurately reading her readiness," she wondered. "Making a difference often does mean assisting with the process of change for influential leaders and their organizations. But maybe I got too wrapped up in my own needs and it skewed my point of view. I know I got really attached to RJ."

Sophia checked the time on her laptop. Since her call with RJ had been so short, she still had about sixty minutes before her next coaching call. She decided to enjoy the beautiful day with a brisk walk around the neighborhood. She could get some fresh air and reflect further on what had just happened.

As she stepped outside into the warmth and light, Sophia felt a twinge of sadness. She really *had* been expecting a yes from RJ. Even though Sophia had plenty of clients to keep her busy, she felt a sense of loss.

As Sophia walked, she recognized the sensation of regret and disappointment which often fueled the voice of her Inner Persecutor. Already she could hear its critical chatter about how she had bungled things with RJ. In the past, Sophia resisted acknowledging her self-critical voice, thinking it was better to ignore it and put it out of her mind. But she had learned it was better not to push away any part of herself, no matter how annoying it might be.

As Sophia walked, she allowed the emotions to flow through her body. She smiled. "If only my neighbors could hear all the stuff I say to myself on my walks!" She wanted to listen now, to hear what her Inner DDT characters had to say. "Okay, folks," she said to them. "I'm listening. Do your worst!"

A gruff, frustrated voice was the first to offer its opinion: "A shorter program and not the full-year commitment would have been more appealing to RJ. Why did you push the yearlong program on her? You should have known that would be too much, too soon for her!" The Inner Persecutor was gathering steam, insistent.

"Plus, you could have offered her a less pricey program. Money may not be an issue for her, but still, that might have been helpful. Why didn't you do that?!"

In a moment her Inner Persecutor continued, more easygoing but still quite concerned: "You know you got invested in RJ and really wanted to coach her, but you didn't protest at all. I bet you could have nudged her into saying yes if you had just pushed a little harder." As she listened to these messages, Sophia was beginning to feel like a Victim to her own internal voices.

Then she recognized the voice of the unhelpful helper, her Inner Rescuer, eager to self-soothe. "You'll feel better if you devour one of those chocolate chip cookies waiting for you back at the house."

Hearing her Inner DDT dialogue had become more comfortable for Sophia since her Sunday afternoon walk a few weeks earlier. She had learned that she could simply listen to these messages without doing anything about them. To her surprise, what they had to say was often useful.

Sophia had once been overwhelmed by these critical inner voices. But now, respecting them and allowing them to make their points seemed to ease their tone and soften their demands. When she paused, listened, and didn't resist them, Sophia found she could trust her best self, her Creator essence, to get curious about their points of view. She could ask herself, "Is there any truth to this? What can I learn from these messages?"

Sophia returned to the house, took up a pen and a sheet of paper, and began writing rapidly. She wanted to record the insights she had gained on her walk. It was true, she had become highly attached to the idea of coaching RJ. She had grown very fond of her. Sophia had formed the belief that a coaching partnership would help free RJ from being ruled by her father's and grandfather's expectations. Sophia had been looking forward to supporting RJ in becoming the kind of leader and person she obviously wanted to be. And she wanted to help RJ get free of the castle of control she had constructed around herself.

"It'll be interesting to hear what Tara thinks about all this," Sophia mused. "She always has great insights."

Sophia put down the pen and paper to refocus. She needed to prepare for her two remaining client calls and wanted to answer all her emails. That way she could really shut down her work during her three days off. "I'll have plenty of time for the inner work soon enough," she thought.

That evening Sophia did her best not to ruminate about RJ's decision.

It was almost time for bed, and the thrill of vacation time was stirring. She needed these upcoming days of relaxation and reconnection with her good friend. Before turning off her computer for the night, Sophia checked her email one last time and found a fun one from Gabe. The subject line was, "Yes, send ASAP!" She opened the email and read his message.

*Dear Mom,*

*What great timing. It is getting chilly here in Colorado. The first snow is on its way next week in the mountains. Only a month or two and we'll be in for great snowboarding! I love the first snow. It always reminds me of the first day of school, only a lot better! Please send the sweatshirts and flannel shirts as soon as possible. I can definitely use them. The other things I would be glad for you to give away. Thanks so much, Mom. Let's talk soon. Love you! Gabe*

*PS. Might as well add my baseball glove too. I am thinking about joining a coed softball team next spring.*

Sophia read Gabe's message a couple more times, smiling at the positive, even childlike exuberance of his writing.

"This is such a great time in your life, Gabe," she said aloud. "It makes me so happy to know you're doing what brings you joy." She paused for a few minutes to savor the love and connection she felt with her son.

\* \* \*

Sophia had planned to allow herself to sleep in the next morning, but she didn't make it past 7:00 a.m. She was excited to get on the road and off to the beach. The drive was four, maybe five hours—just long enough to disconnect from home and work, but not so long it was tiring. After a quick breakfast, she was back in her bedroom, packing a few last items into her weekend bag, when her phone rang. It was Tara.

"Hey Tara. I'm just finishing up packing. Can't wait to see you!"

"That's why I am calling," Tara said. Her voice sounded solemn. Sophia could hear that something wasn't right.

Tara continued, "I hoped to see you, too, but I'm not sure it will work this weekend. My brother, Paco, has taken a sudden turn for the worse this week. This last week has been very difficult for Paco. His remission didn't last long . . . he is suddenly in an acute stage now."

Sophia said, "Oh Tara, I'm so sorry to hear that. It must be a difficult time for you and your family. Being with him is so important. And Paco is such a kind person."

"Thank you, Sophia," Tara said. "Right now, he's in an outpatient clinic receiving another unit of blood. We're hopeful this will make a difference as it has in the past. But he's very anemic, he's having a difficult time breathing, and he's very weak.

"Our family is circling around him," said Tara. "Paco's big spirit is so present. My heart aches." She paused. "Text me when you arrive and I will let you know if I'll be able to join you."

"I will, Tara," said Sophia. "And please don't worry about me. Thank you for your call. My heart goes out to Paco and your family . . . and for your journey with him."

"Thank you," said Tara. "Drive safe, my friend."

Sophia hung up. Her excitement had turned to sadness for Tara, Paco, and their family. "Another chance to learn about letting go of expectations."

# 12

# Disappointment and Dynamic Tension

After a pleasant drive, Sophia arrived at her familiar beach cottage home-away-from-home at around five in the evening. She had taken her time, stopping at familiar spots along the way. Whenever she drove to the beach, Sophia made sure to pull over at the lookout point where she could enjoy a view of the vast shipping lanes where jumbo container ships sailed in and out of the Port of Seattle. She usually stopped at her favorite café for lunch, and after that she visited the small state park just off the main road, known for its walking trails that weave through a grove of giant red cedars.

When she arrived at the cottage, Sophia parked under the carport, retrieved her bags from the trunk, then located the house key in the lockbox. Once inside, she set down her bags and stood admiring the cozy living room. "This place immediately puts me in a calm mood," she thought. "So good to be here again."

She carried her luggage to the bedroom, then headed back to the car to retrieve the ice chest. She had packed the cooler with food, snacks, sparkling water, a bottle of her favorite chardonnay, and a few other goodies. After relaxing on the couch for a few minutes, she pulled her phone from her bag and texted Tara.

*I just arrived at the beach house, Tara. Thinking of you and your family lots. Let me know what works best for you.* She added two red heart emojis.

After an hour, Sophia still hadn't heard from Tara. Feeling hungry, she began planning what would be easy to fix but tasty. As she bustled about the small kitchen, dinner quickly materialized: a platter of sliced salami and cheeses, olives, grapes, and a mini baguette. She poured herself a glass of wine. "If Tara stops by tonight, there will be plenty for her as well," Sophia said to herself, hoping to hear from her friend at any minute.

She carried her feast to the front porch and sat down in the rocking chair—her favorite, still there after all these years. The beach wasn't visible from the cottage, but she reveled in the cool, salty air and the sound of seagulls squawking in the distance.

Another hour passed and still no word from Tara. Probably not a good sign. She thought of Paco and the challenge he was facing, knowing that his blood disease carried a "terminal illness" label.

"Isn't life eventually terminal for everyone, though?" Sophia thought, then immediately criticized herself: "That's an insensitive thought. He's Tara's little brother, and this must be so hard for her. For everyone in her family."

It was getting dark now and Sophia was starting to feel the fatigue from her trip. She cleaned up her dishes, poured herself another half glass of wine, and put the meat and cheese back in the fridge. It was still early, but she knew sleep wasn't far off. Before heading to the bedroom, she found the novel she had packed. How nice it would be to have plenty of reading time this weekend!

After three chapters, Sophia reached over to turn out the light. Just then she heard the ping of a new text. She had forgotten to bring the phone with her to the nightstand. "That's good," she thought. "Guess I'm already starting to disengage and relax." She got out of bed and found her phone on the kitchen table. Tara had texted,

*Sophia, so happy you arrived okay. Paco has rallied and it appears the blood transfusion is working its magic. I want to spend tomorrow morning with him and then plan to see you in the afternoon. Let's text again in the morning. Sleep well, my friend.*

Sophia stared at the text and smiled contentedly at Tara's good news. She placed her phone on the charger and went back to bed. After one more chapter of her novel she turned off the little bedside lamp, grateful for the silence.

Just before dawn the next morning, Sophia carried her cup of coffee and her journal to the front porch rocking chair. After only a few minutes of writing, it became clear that RJ's decision to say no to coaching was still on her mind. "I thought I had let go of that," she muttered to herself. "Must not have, though, since I'm still writing about it this morning!"

She closed her journal and sat rocking peacefully, enjoying the fresh morning air as the sun's bright golden rays began to emerge on the horizon.

"After breakfast I'll take the trail to the beach," she thought. She could hardly wait to see Tara.

After Sophia returned from her beach exploration, Tara texted that Paco had had a good night's rest and that she had been sitting with him all morning. She added, *I'll join you around 3 p.m. at the cottage, if that's okay.* Sophia immediately texted back: *Yes! Perfect. See you then.*

\* \* \*

As she heard Tara's car pulling into the driveway, Sophia waved from the porch, then hurried outside to open the driver's side door, delighted to be welcoming her favorite friend.

"Tara, it is *so* good to see you! Thank you for making time this afternoon," Sophia said.

"Of course!" said Tara. "It's good for me to get out for my daily walk and take a break, even though being with Paco is so important right now. And it is special that you are here. I'm happy to see you, Sophia." Tara looked up and all around. "The afternoon is bright and warm," she said. "I'd like to go right down to the beach! How's that sound?"

"Absolutely. I'm ready," Sophia said, zipping up her vest.

The ocean breeze had dissipated. Low tide meant there would be plenty of sandy beach for walking. Tara and Sophia both preferred walking at low tide. When the water receded, it revealed rocks covered in barnacles and shore crabs scurrying away from low-swooping seagulls hoping to catch dinner. Sprightly plovers hopped around in the shallow surf.

Tara seemed to walk slower than usual, and after the two friends had strolled along for a while in silence, she shared her sadness. Even though she had known, when Paco was diagnosed two years earlier, that her brother probably would live only a few more years, Tara still felt a deep grief. Close in age, Paco and Tara had grown up together and were as close as ever. As small children they had spent many afternoons playing hide-and-seek, and later as young teenagers they had remained best friends, once even going on a double date. But what Tara remembered most fondly was being with her brother on or near the water, the two of them teasing about whose fishing catch weighed in heavier, and the silent hours spent rhythmically paddling in silence in Paco's canoe.

Tara looked up at Sophia. "How's Gabe?" she asked. "Is he doing all right on his own in Colorado?" Sophia was happy to report that her son was doing very well and had approved of her gift of the birthday mug.

"And how are things going with the intriguing new client you told me about a few weeks ago?" Tara asked. "You shared that she was presenting a challenge or two?"

"Or two," chuckled Sophia, rolling her eyes. "Thanks for asking. Actually, she chose not to renew our contract. I'll just leave it at that for now."

After they had walked a bit further down the beach, suddenly Tara reached out and gently nudged Sophia's waist, signaling her to stop. Sophia realized she had been walking with her head down, watching her steps in the sand. Now she looked up.

"Do you see those two eagles?" Tara whispered. "Over there, to your right. See how they're feasting on the exposed low tides?"

Tara took in a breath and gently exhaled. "They grace us today with their power and sacred presence." As Tara spoke, Sophia felt the words. A shiver ran through her body like a sparkling rain.

"I guess it's no surprise to see the eagles today. The tide is so low. Several are living in this area and there's a large nest in the Douglas firs over there." Tara pointed to the stand of giant trees not far from the shore. Sophia could see an eagle's nest in the top branches of one.

"Sophia, did you know that the Indigenous meaning of Paco's name is *Eagle*?" asked Tara. "Since he was a little boy, Paco has always loved watching his namesake bird. It is a gift today, to experience them here, so close. To us, the eagle and its feather symbolize courage, wisdom, and strength. I've often seen that strength in Paco."

Sophia and Tara watched the eagles in silence for some time.

Tara said, "My people appreciate so many qualities of Eagle. One is keen eyesight. From thousands of feet away, Eagle can clearly see its prey. That's where the term *eagle eye* comes from. But what Paco loves most, he has said, is how Eagle, unlike other birds, will never surrender."

Tara continued, "Seeing the eagles reminds me of the time Paco and I watched an eagle hunting. I was about twelve and Paco was ten. We were playing near the water and saw some ducks swimming in the shallows. We watched those ducks for several minutes when suddenly an eagle dove from high in the sky at lightning speed, and with its sharp talons it grabbed the back of one of the ducks." Tara brought her hand down fast in a grasping motion to show the speed with which the eagle had accomplished its aim.

"That duck struggled mightily for the longest time," said Tara, "even forcing the eagle into the surf as it fought back. But the eagle managed to stay upright and mostly out of the water. And then it started frantically flapping its wings, again and again and again." Tara's eyes shone as she relived the story.

"Their combined weight was taking them both underwater. They would roll up above the surface, and then they'd go back under again. But finally, the eagle was able to lift its strong wings all the way up out of the water, and it began flapping. It took a while, but the eagle's strength lifted them both just inches above the water line, with the duck still quacking and struggling, hanging from the eagle's talons.

"That eagle slowly gained altitude. Paco and I could hardly believe it," said Tara, telling the story with her arms, lifting them gradually up in the air for effect.

"By the time the eagle reached land, it had risen just a few feet above our heads. Then it landed on the large, low branch of a nearby tree. Somehow the eagle kept its hold on that duck, which was still quacking and struggling. Eagle had the wisdom to rest for a minute, knowing it needed to regain its strength before it could fly all the way up to its nest carrying that duck. At last, it flew. An amazing sight—nature feeding the cycle of life and death, right before our young eyes."

Tara smiled. "My brother and I have shared many great times. That was only one day of many."

She paused a moment, pensive, eyeing the water's edge, and continued.

"Eagles never stop fighting—never let go of their prey. That is another reason why Eagle is so greatly revered. And it's why I feel that Paco continues to fight his battle with this disease. We all know that in the end his body will return to Mother Earth. But for now, he fights hard to be alive, to be with us."

Tara sighed, yet now she no longer looked tired. Her shoulders were relaxed, her head high. Sophia wondered if the eagles had somehow appeared to help Tara remember that story, to give her a chance to share with a friend how very much she loved her brother.

Tara saw Sophia's serious look and laughed. "Now I want to hear more about what's going on with you!"

As they continued walking, Sophia opened up, sharing her disappointment about RJ deciding against the long-term coaching contract she had offered. But she was quick to add her good news as well—including how Gabe and his dad had grown closer over the years.

The two women gradually made their way back to the trail and up to the cottage. Inside, Tara checked her phone. Seeing no new message about Paco, she accepted Sophia's invitation to stay for dinner.

Sophia poured her friend a glass of wine and they chatted happily, toasting their time together. Sharing more details of her last session with RJ, Sophia got a sudden inspiration. Retrieving her notebook from the table, she said, "Tara, I just realized something: the dynamic tension model might help me understand this lingering disappointment I'm feeling about RJ's decision to quit coaching."

"That's a creative idea," Tara said. "How about I take notes so you're free to share?" She reached out to take the notebook.

"Of course. Please do!" said Sophia.

"Okay if I ask you a couple of questions?" asked Tara, taking Sophia's pen.

"Of course. I always love it when you step into the Coach role," Sophia said.

"When you reflect back on your feelings about coaching with RJ, what did you want?" asked Tara.

"I wanted RJ to go further with coaching. I was positive that coaching could support her and her team in directly addressing the complaints she had voiced to me. I was sure she would grow personally, as well as become a better leader, if she changed some of her reactive habits. I was really looking forward to the opportunity to influence a leader who's in a position to positively influence others."

"We all get attached to the things we want, so that's understandable. Tara drew a small circle on the upper left side of the page, then wrote, *Attached to coaching RJ and changing some of her reactive habits.* Does that fairly represent your focus?"

"Yes, I guess it does . . . although until now I had no idea how strongly I was attached to RJ saying yes."

"Okay." Tara returned to her drawing. A couple of inches below the first circle, she drew a second circle. "This bottom circle represents the reality at the time that you were focused on RJ saying yes. And the current reality is that RJ has said *no* to coaching, correct?"

"Yes, that is the reality," agreed Sophia, "but there's a lot more to my current reality than RJ saying no. For example, one part of my reality is that I started coming up with ideas about how to change the contract and resubmit it to RJ. I've been thinking about calling her back to talk her into a contract with a shorter timeframe, and maybe reduce the price. Another part of the reality is that I stayed awake for a few hours in the middle of the night feeling upset and disappointed."

"All right, we'll summarize that here." Tara wrote in the bottom circle, *RJ said no. Sophia is upset and awake at night, wants to convince her to say yes.*

"Does that fairly represent what you said?" she asked.

Sophia looked at the words on the circles. She was feeling upset all over again.

Tara interrupted her ruminations. "So, what do we have here? Two points pulling in opposite directions. In one direction is your desire to coach RJ. In the other direction are your reactive thoughts and emotions connected to her saying no. They pull in these two opposite directions, creating a lot of tension."

Sophia had a thought. "Dynamic tension is exactly the right name for the energy, in the gap between what I want and what I have. I'm feeling the tension right now as I relive what happened." She picked up the pen and drew a squiggly line going upward from the bottom circle to the top circle, representing the dynamic tension.

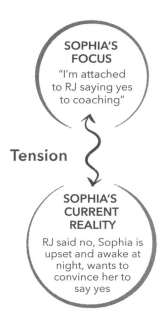

**SOPHIA'S FOCUS**

"I'm attached to RJ saying yes to coaching"

Tension

**SOPHIA'S CURRENT REALITY**

RJ said no, Sophia is upset and awake at night, wants to convince her to say yes

*Diagram 6. Dynamic Tension 1*

Tara smiled. "I'm thinking of the way eagles fly into the wind, how they use that pressure to soar high on its current. We can do the same thing, if we are mindful of the way our thoughts create the tension we feel. It is important to ask ourselves, 'How am I relating to the natural tension that's happening all the time in life? Am I flowing with it, making good use of it the way Eagle does, or am I letting it overwhelm me?'

"Sophia," she asked, "how are you relating to the tension in the gap between expecting RJ to say yes, and the reality that she said no to more coaching?"

"Not well at all. I felt the tension in my gut and chest as soon as I hung up with her. I'm feeling it again right now. It's a mixture of sadness, loss, disappointment, and worry. I heard my Inner Persecutor complaining and criticizing the way I handled the situation.

"I also looked for a Rescuer by staying busy, not allowing myself to feel all those uncomfortable feelings that sometimes trigger me to eat a lot of pastries." Sophia recalled how, on her neighborhood walk, she had felt a strong urge to go home and devour a chocolate chip cookie to soothe herself.

"And . . . I felt like a Victim, powerless to change RJ's decision. I was experiencing all three of the DDT roles at once!"

"An important insight, Sophia. The key is learning to relax with that, even when it's uncomfortable. If we don't, the DDT roles will keep doing their dance, trying to manage our anxiety. This is so difficult to remember when we're in the grip of the DDT."

Tara spoke softly. "Sophia, did you know that eagles are just about the only birds that love storms? When storm winds come up, all the other birds try to flee, but the eagles fly right in there, using the wind current to glide higher. Instead of resisting the wind, they relax and conserve their energy. They allow the tension of those storm currents to lift them up and carry them along."

"Tara," Sophia interjected, "I just realized something. I am in a problem relationship with RJ's decision. I am making a problem out of RJ saying no!" Sophia stared at the graphic, her insights gaining steam.

"And whenever I label anything a problem—you know, when I *really don't want* something—my inner state turns anxious and heavy and just . . . really difficult to work with. And then I want to numb the uncomfortable feelings. That DDT dance is exactly what I did when RJ said no!"

Sophia paused. "What if . . . I let go of my wish that RJ had said yes, and changed my focus to just being the coach, the person, I want to be? If I let go of that attachment, what would my *new* outcome focus be?"

She looked at Tara's dynamic tension circles. "And then, where would my new outcome go, in the graphic here?" Her pen hovered over the page.

Sophia drew a new circle, a few inches to the right of Tara's drawing. As she drew, she felt an excited, bubbly energy. She was shifting her focus on a problem into a focus on a desired outcome. Wasn't this an essential skill for any coach—learning to change from a focus on problems to a focus on outcomes? And yet she had forgotten to apply the same principle for herself!

Above the new circle she wrote: *What is the outcome I desire?* The answer came almost immediately.

In the center of the circle, Sophia wrote her new desired outcome: *I trust my client and her process and have faith that she will change when she is ready.*

"Reminds me to practice what I preach," Sophia mused, still looking at the paper.

"Okay, so if my new desired outcome is to trust my client and their process," she said, "what's my current reality?" Sophia reflected a moment, pen poised. "Actually, it's really simple, isn't it?" She drew a straight line down to the circle below.

"My current reality is that I can get triggered sometimes and forget the principles I value as a coach.

I may slip up, but I won't give up. I will acknowledge and foster my Creator essence."

"Okay!" encouraged Tara.

Sophia began writing her new current reality in the circle at the lower right of the page. Before finishing, she paused and said, "I'm going to reframe that last sentence. Instead of 'I won't give up' . . . "She wrote the words as she said them out loud: "I am committed to continuously learning."

"*These* two points pull in opposite directions, too, don't they?" said Sophia. "One statement is pulling toward learning to trust my client's process. Then, the truth that I sometimes get triggered and forget my own coaching principles—that's pulling in the other direction. With those two points in opposition, there is still dynamic tension. But the feeling of that tension is completely different," she said, feeling jubilant.

"I feel calmer *and* more trusting right now. I can be patient with myself and give myself a break when I slip up. The feeling I got from the other approach was full of heavy energy. With this shift in my focus, I really care about this outcome, and the energy is more positive and uplifting," Sophia exclaimed.

"Thanks, Tara, for listening . . . and for your great questions. That was amazing."

"You asked most of the questions yourself, my friend!" Tara laughed.

"I kind of surprised myself, I guess—in just a few seconds I shifted my whole focus! And I already feel a real shift in my emotional inner state, too. I can relax into *this* tension with a lot more ease."

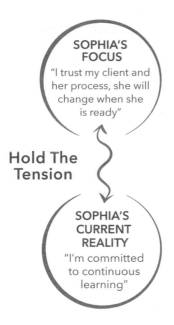

*Diagram 7. Dynamic Tension 2*

"Beautiful insight, Sophia." Tara smiled. "You rediscovered the secret to creating the life you want. Learning to ease into the tension—instead of resisting or rejecting it—actually propels you forward. The way Eagle does, sensing the tension in the wind and using it to fly along with the storm.

"It isn't always obvious, or easy, to shift our focus from a problem to our desired outcome," added Tara. "We humans are usually focusing on what's *wrong*." She made a theatrical pouting face, and Sophia chuckled.

"If we label everything we encounter in life as a problem, we're going to feel afraid of problems most of the time. Even though we create those problems in our own mind! When we reframe, as you say, toward the positive outcome that we want, then positive feelings are bound to show up. We're happier when we're focusing on what we care about. And that makes sense, doesn't it?

"Just that one shift can change our whole relationship to life—the Big Circle that surrounds all of these!" Tara made a circle with her arms as though holding all of the experience represented in the drawings.

Sophia put the pen down. In Tara's face she saw strength and great wisdom. She appreciated her friend beyond measure but knew it was time to wrap up their visit.

"I value our times together," said Tara, glancing out the window. The sun was dipping behind the treetops. "Time for me to go now. I want to check in on Paco again. And I plan to see you tomorrow!" she added brightly.

"Oh, and Sophia, I almost forgot. I spoke with Ted earlier. He'd love to meet us for a walk tomorrow afternoon."

# 13

## Wrestling with Life

After a deep sleep, Sophia woke and was surprised to see it was already after eight o'clock. She got up quickly and walked into the living room. The early sun shone brightly through the east-facing window. Thousands of tiny dust particles danced in the air, reflecting the light. "I love the mornings here," she thought, feeling the sun's warmth on her skin as she chose a tranquil spot to place her meditation cushion.

She scanned the spare cottage. There was the watercolor painting of a young girl playing on the beach. On the end table next to the familiar armchair, a sad plant was beginning to wither a little. "Must give that one a drink of water," she thought. The threadbare armchair was no less cozy for its fuzzy state. In it she had spent untold hours gazing out the window, creatively daydreaming. She felt at home here, centered and safe. As she watched the sparkling particles floating in midair, she thought, "This light is nourishing. And it reveals." As it bounced off mere specks of dust, the sunlight created fascinating patterns.

Sophia placed her cushion on the floor and sat in the familiar cross-legged pose, her back resting against the front of the couch. It had been nearly ten years since Sophia attended her first silent meditation retreat and committed to a daily meditation practice. While at first it had felt awkward for her to be with others without talking, she soon found it a relief. The retreat offered her the practice of slowing down her busy mind and the space to listen to her own thoughts. Once she began paying attention to her internal chatter, Sophia was shocked to witness the parade of complaints, judgments, and senseless commentary marching through her mind. It was even more frustrating to see how she judged even her own judgmental thoughts! After a few days, however, her mind grew quieter, and she was able to simply watch her inner dialogue come and go without taking it all so seriously.

In her meditation class, the teacher suggested adopting a metaphor to put distance between herself and her repetitive inner monologue. Sophia had chosen the metaphor of a movie theater. She visualized sitting in a safe seat watching the movie of her life. As she watched the movie on her mental screen, she felt less involved in the drama. Thanks to that retreat, her contemplative practice, and that comforting movie metaphor, she had found calm amidst her inner chaos.

As she continued to meditate daily, Sophia became more familiar with the thoughts, emotions, and subtle sensations constantly competing for her attention. Gradually she had become willing to feel all of her emotions, even the most difficult ones. She had begun to feel less afraid of her fear, less ashamed of her anger and sadness, and less anxious when she experienced anxiety.

Growing up in a family where emotions were hidden, Sophia avoided expressing her feelings, fearing they might upset others, cause conflict, or worse, overwhelm her. She developed a habit of pleasing and accommodating others, which won her friends but didn't make her any more comfortable with her emotions. Later, as an adult, Sophia often felt dismay at her inability to express herself clearly and truly. During her marriage to Dan, she eventually withdrew so thoroughly and covered her inner life so well that, at the end, she hardly recognized herself.

Sophia had acquired an internal message that constantly admonished her to "be nice." There was nothing wrong with being nice, of course, except when it suppressed her authentic voice and her joyful creativity. Meditation taught her that she could afford to relax and allow herself to feel, that the uncomfortable feelings would run their course. With this relaxed awareness, Sophia learned that she didn't need to explain to herself or anyone else why her feelings were coming up. By not stirring up a lot of mental activity, by simply observing her thoughts and emotions, Sophia developed a welcome capability to stay present with life's many experiences as they emerged. This was a game-changing gift of her meditation practice. Of course, she still had to show up daily to develop and claim that gift, but she would forever be grateful for this rejuvenating habit.

But sometimes, such as when her client RJ rejected the long-term coaching contract, Sophia could get triggered. The conversation with Tara about dynamic tension was a breakthrough that was now supporting her to reframe her focus. During this morning's mediation, Sophia practiced continuing to relax and become acclimated to that new focus: letting go and trusting her client's process.

After a half hour of meditation, Sophia showered and made breakfast. On the drive down, she had bought fresh eggs and a loaf of homemade bread at the farmer's market, with just this moment in mind. She sliced two generous pieces of the bread and slid them into the toaster. The delicate aroma flooded the cottage. As soon as her slices popped up, she spread them with creamy farm butter and took a bite. Delicious! Leaning against the kitchen counter, she held a slice of bread just below her nose and inhaled the toasty fragrance. "This is a whole other kind of meditation," she thought, and she savored every bite.

Sophia cherished the slow unfolding of her mornings at the cottage. No need to rush to work, check emails, write proposals, or plant herself in front of a computer screen. Here, she basked in the blissful freedom from routine.

And today was special. Ted would be meeting them for a midafternoon walk on the beach. During her video calls with Tara, Sophia occasionally received news of Ted, but now it had been several years since their last visit, and she was eager to see him. Whenever Sophia spent time with Ted, she came away feeling that she understood herself better, though she couldn't always pinpoint how it had happened.

She had met Ted fifteen years earlier, during her first retreat to the beach cottage. Back then, Sophia had been a woman in crisis, recovering from a broken marriage and wrestling with deep self-doubt. All those years ago, her new friend Tara had kindly introduced Sophia to Ted. Ever since she had met these two extraordinary people, Sophia's life had taken profound and interesting turns.

Ted had been the first to introduce Sophia to the Dreaded Drama Triangle, the DDT. She had been stunned to realize how, for years, she had unconsciously viewed herself as a Victim, powerless in the face of life's challenges. Sophia had learned from Ted that when anyone falls into the Victim role, their dreams are put on the back burner, in some cases so far back that those dreams are no longer even discernable. As the ability to dream recedes, Ted had explained, the Victim mentality takes over and people begin to sleepwalk through life, forgetting their innate power to be the person they most long to be. Eventually, he said, this energy pattern and the ways of thinking that go with it could cause that longing itself to go numb. It was Ted who had helped Sophia see that although she had lost touch with it, she, like all human beings, still had the capacity to grow and evolve into her very best self, and to fulfill her deepest dreams and desires.

That week so many years ago, walking the beach with Tara and Ted, Sophia had felt both shocked and renewed. She had unwittingly silenced her voice and suppressed her spirit! At the same time, locked into the ways she had learned to survive, Sophia couldn't even imagine what it might feel like to thrive. Ted had helped Sophia discover how she often entered the DDT through the Victim role, but then quickly took on the role of Rescuer, adopting pleasing behaviors to placate others, especially her husband, Dan. Sophia had believed that if she made other people happy, that should make her happy, too. By the time she met Ted, she had spent nearly half her life stuck in the Rescuer role.

Sophia liked that she cared about helping people, but she had been forced to admit that lately her efforts to please had begun to feel more like drudgery—a duty rather than a choice. Others' needs always seemed to come before hers, until eventually she could hardly remember what her own needs were! Sophia's focus on pleasing others had become an automatic response; the desire to please had become a compulsion.

After that crucial insight, Sophia gradually learned she could live life on her own terms, saying yes where appropriate, but also saying no when that was warranted. This change presented a tough challenge for Sophia, who had long acquiesced to her husband's strong personality and tendency to dominate. Saying no had never been an option in that relationship, or at least it seemed that way at the time.

Her weekend of beach walks with Tara and Ted had set Sophia on a new path. Step by step, through regular video calls with Tara, who generously offered her mentorship and support, Sophia gained insight and built up her confidence. She began to take full responsibility for her thoughts and actions instead of seeing herself as a Victim of circumstance. Best of all, she began to believe in herself. Sophia had made the shift from being stuck in the DDT to becoming a conscious Creator of her own life.

Sophia smiled to herself. "That Ted is a rock star!" she thought. "He helped me rediscover my passions and everything I care about. His teachings even helped me become the mother I wanted to be for Gabe. But today I'm in a new place, a little wiser and definitely older. I just turned sixty!"

Sophia now felt a sense of security and independence she couldn't have imagined when she first met Ted. No longer merely grateful to get through the day, she felt strong. Making a meaningful contribution was her focus now.

But despite all that good growth, as Sophia witnessed the complex problems throughout the world, at times she almost felt like a Victim again. There was a creeping sense of powerlessness over it all, and the uncertainty made it less clear how best to contribute her gifts.

"I'm sure Ted will have some helpful suggestions for relating to these new challenges we're all facing," she thought, renewing her excitement.

Sophia could already feel the pull toward the wooded trail that meandered from her cottage out to the spot on the beach where she would meet up with Tara and Ted. Their traditional meeting place! But just as Sophia had gathered up her things and closed the door to go, she got a text from Tara.

*Sorry for the late notice. I want to spend a little more time with Paco this afternoon. I will meet you and Ted in an hour, at the big boulder just below the cliff. Until then . . . :-)*

"Good for her," thought Sophia, remembering her own struggle to stop the old habit of people-pleasing at her own expense. Tara had no hesitation about changing plans when she needed to.

Sophia texted back,

*Sounds good, Tara. Ted and I will have a walk and see you later. Enjoy your time with Paco.*

Sophia put on a light jacket and hurried out the door. She headed briskly down the neatly marked trail, picking up her pace as she went. When she nearly bumped into another hiker coming around a curve in the trail, she slowed down, then stopped. "Look at me. So excited that I'm forgetting to watch where I'm going." She resumed her pace, attending to every step.

Her first sign of Ted was the hat. "Is that the same one he wore the day we met, years ago?" She chuckled to herself. But as she drew closer, the straw sun hat was unmistakable. Floppy in the back to cover his neck, with a flat brim that spread out in front to protect his face. Supremely practical, but certainly not meant to impress.

"Ted!" she yelled. Sophia surged ahead, almost running, until she caught up with her friend. "I'm so happy to see you!" He turned toward her with that gentleness she so fondly remembered. A few more wrinkles on his face, but the same welcoming smile. He opened his hands, gesturing her closer, and they fell into a long bear hug.

Ted stood back and paused, taking her in. He said softly, "Sophia, my dear. How are you? You look lovely. It's so good to be with you again."

"I'm well," said Sophia, somewhat breathlessly. "Yes, doing well, considering all of life's challenges. I am healthy and enjoying my work and home. Gabe—you remember my son, Gabe—has grown into a wonderful young man, out on his own now and working in Boulder, doing the things he loves."

Sophia glowed as she gave her report, then said, "And you, Ted. Tell me about you. You're staying healthy and taking care of yourself?"

Ted nodded his appreciation for her concern. "I'm doing well, as well!" He smiled. "Fully retired now, living here at the beach house a couple of miles up. Friends visit from time to time, and we have marvelous conversations. And I have more time now to read." He paused. "More time to make sense of life." He chuckled. "Not sure I have any new insights, but I'm certainly enjoying myself."

"And how is your retreat going, Sophia dear? I know these are important times of reflection for you. What's been on your mind?"

Sophia smiled and glanced away briefly. "Oh, that's a big question, Ted. I am wrestling with life again, I guess. Kind of a new chapter for me. I'm wondering, with the years I have left, how I can make a real contribution. The world's problems seem so large that I've been feeling unsure where to focus my deep desire to be of service in the world. I've been hard on myself lately—guess you could say I'm in a problem relationship with myself and have been getting stuck in my Inner DDT."

"Oh my," said Ted, softly. "Please say more, dear. What's that like?"

"Well, I'd just like to stop judging my life based on what I've achieved or haven't achieved. I can't believe I'm still doing that, but I am. I keep measuring what I have fixed or haven't fixed about the world, according to how many influential leaders I have or haven't coached. It sounds silly as I say it. I need a new way to measure my contribution.

"And I want to feel *fulfilled*," she said. "Is it selfish to want that, when the world's problems are so enormous?"

She took a deep breath and let out a long sigh. "Oh my, Ted. You always have this effect on me. We just said hello and I'm already going on and on about trying to change the world. And myself!"

Ted nodded with a little smile. "Life is full of mystery. It is natural to want to find our place in it, to want to contribute to a better world."

Sophia jumped in: "What has *your* journey been like, Ted? It's pretty clear you have found your place."

Ted seemed pleased to philosophize a bit more. "We all have unique stories, don't we? My big changes took hold in my middle years when I first started shifting my viewpoint—which after all, is just a view from one point," he said, chuckling at the turn of phrase.

"At that time, I had suffered a great deal by constantly trying to fix things that lay outside my control. In those days I believed it was only possible to change things by focusing on problems 'out there.' I didn't succeed in fixing anything, but I did become exhausted! At last, I realized that I really only have power over one thing . . . my own thinking!" He smiled. "I can only change what is in my own heart and mind, starting with how I relate to myself.

"That's when I shifted my perspective from struggling against the world to loving and appreciating the Creator essence in myself and everyone else. And I still feel that is the first and most important work we can do. Because how can we love and trust others, and work for a just world, if we don't care about ourselves?"

"Please say more about that, Ted," said Sophia. "How did you come to believe in your Creator essence? And how did you know that it exists in all beings?"

"Well, it wasn't an overnight awareness, I can tell you. It was more like a gradual knowing. It grew over time, I guess. Against all odds, really, because I was born into a family that taught me that I and all other human beings are born with a flawed nature.

"But as I grew older, that belief stopped feeling true. I began to spend more time in nature—the beautiful forests and beaches of the Pacific Northwest," said Ted, gesturing toward a stand of evergreen trees on the overlooking ridge.

"I could feel the Creator essence pulsating through all of nature, and then, slowly, I began to feel it within myself as well. Not because someone told me that was true—I knew it because I felt it in this body," he said, patting his chest.

"I remember one moment in particular. I was hiking through a thick forest—I was probably forty years old then. I'd been tromping along for about an hour and hadn't met any other hikers. It was just me and the tall trees, taking in the fresh air and the birds chirping. And suddenly I felt a cascade of calm flowing from the top of my head, down through my chest and heart space, all the way out through my fingers and down through my legs. My fingers and toes were tingling and I felt a kind of lightness.

"I felt suddenly open and curious about everything. *Connected* to everything. I felt . . . *alive!*" Ted laughed a big belly laugh and threw his arms out wide.

"I've never forgotten that experience," he said. "Right then I knew I had goodness within me, that there was nothing fundamentally wrong with me at all. From then on, I decided I would cultivate that feeling. I began to think of it as my Creator essence. As Life itself . . . living me!" Ted looked suddenly young; his cheeks flushed.

He continued, "I began to follow that direct knowing, my Creator essence, as my guide, and as a result I became a very different sort of person. Fear no longer ruled my thoughts or told me I was bad. More and more I began to appreciate the feeling and the mystery of being alive. I just *fell in love* with being human."

A calmness came over Sophia. "What a beautiful realization, Ted. To love being fully human."

"Well, it's a good thing I decided to love it," Ted laughed, "because that's what I am. There really weren't any other options available!" He winked.

"Please say more, Ted," Sophia urged. "It's so good for me to hear this right now."

"Well, it all just kind of progressed from there. I kept tapping into that feeling. And gradually I understood that all my anxiety was coming from my thoughts. *That* was an eye-opener! I began to see that when I focused on problems, then, sure as the world, anxious and fearful emotions would surface in response to those 'problem' thoughts. And then I had an epiphany: my thoughts were just momentary—and so in the very next moment, I could change them!

"Along with that, I had a second discovery: Most actions I had taken in my life up to that point had been in response to my anxious feelings. All along I had believed my anxiety was a result of the problems I saw 'out there.' But no! It was *my relationship* to those 'problems' that was causing my strong emotional reactions.

"Life changed rapidly for me after that," said Ted. "I paid more attention to my thoughts right in the moment. And I would intentionally change those thoughts if they weren't supporting me to be at my best. I learned to *choose* my thoughts."

Ted paused to watch a seagull skimming the surface of the water. "I also started reading more and hanging out with folks who studied human development. I met people who liked to translate complex ideas into simple frameworks to help others. I discovered Dr. Stephen Karpman's description of the Drama Triangle, which, as you know, I nicknamed the *Dreaded* Drama Triangle—with its roles of Victim, Persecutor, and Rescuer. It really helped, being able to name those reactive DDT patterns. But I sensed there were other roles at work in human beings, too, that could lead us out of all that unnecessary drama. More positive roles, based on our Creator essence.

"When I pondered the positive alternatives to the DDT, those new roles came to life," said Ted. "The ones we now know as the TED* roles—Creator, Challenger, and Coach—that represent the positive, true essence of who we really are as humans . . . even though we forget them sometimes.

"Well, that's the gist of my story!" Ted proclaimed with a slight bow. He placed his hands over his heart and, with a big smile, said, "Thanks for listening, my dear."

# 14

## The Creator Essence

What a fascinating journey you've had, Ted. Thank you for sharing that," said Sophia. "And I know what you mean: The DDT is an amazing tool for self-discovery. When I started to see how I bounced around the Drama Triangle, from one role to another, it was such a relief to be able to name those patterns of behavior. After that, I had an easier time accepting those patterns as a normal part of my human experience. Once I realized I could have a different kind of relationship with them, I stopped being afraid of those parts of myself—and then my Creator, Challenger, and Coach parts naturally emerged."

Still walking, Sophia nudged up against Ted's shoulder and gently took his arm. His big oilskin coat was soft with wear. He smiled with affection and squeezed her hand.

Sophia continued. "But sometimes I worry that we won't ever get things right in this world. That we human beings may not figure out how to live together peacefully and live in harmony with the planet. We are billions of people and our population is steadily growing, yet we still don't seem to be focused on living together in right relationship. We're still stuck in a system of winners and losers. And the winners create systems that maintain their advantage over everyone else."

Ted listened intently as she continued. "I worry that, as a person of considerable privilege, I'm unaware of the ways I may be helping sustain the system that excludes so many. I'm getting more and more uncomfortable with these feelings, but frankly, I'm not sure what to do about it."

"Sophia, the uncomfortable feelings you're having are common in everyone's life. We all feel frustrated and powerless sometimes. If you judge yourself, thinking you're wrong for feeling sad or even furious about these things, you will surely plant the seeds of the DDT."

Sophia nodded, taking it in. "I know that's true. Every day I say to myself, 'I want to stop feeling this way. I want to stop the thoughts that evoke these emotions.' Because I've realized these past few weeks that I repeat those same thoughts to myself over and over without getting anywhere. Do I just have to learn to be comfortable with uncomfortable feelings?"

They had walked quite a ways now, out onto the sandy beach. Not far off Sophia could see the big boulder where they planned to meet Tara. Nearby a woman and two young boys sat on a patchwork of colorful beach towels, happily chewing on sandwiches. A father and daughter played at the water's edge, batting a beach ball back and forth.

Ted said, "Well, yes, actually it is good to learn to accept discomfiting feelings. Of course, pushing them away may *seem* to work for a while. And it's easy enough to suppress those feelings by getting involved with email, social media, alcohol or drugs, endless sports, constant work, video games, shopping. There are so many distractions available!" Ted gestured emphatically, and so did his hat. His voice and the floppy straw brim were somehow soothing, and Sophia relaxed a little.

"Yet those thoughts you don't want and the difficult feelings that go with them will keep cropping up, the more you try to push them away. When things get really tough, what happens? Those uncomfortable feelings become even more insistent—just like that beach ball."

Ted gestured toward the young girl playing in the water.

"Like a beach ball?!" Sophia wasn't following.

The girl was now waist-deep in the shallow waves, her two arms focused on their task.

"See how hard she is trying to push the beach ball under the water and keep it there? She's pushing it down . . . ah, now she is trying to sit on it! Oops, there it goes, popping right up again." Ted laughed heartily, and the brim of his hat jiggled.

He turned to Sophia. "Did you see how the ball shot up even higher the harder she tried to push it down?"

She nodded. Sophia was beginning to get the drift of the metaphor, and it was fun to see Ted enjoying himself so much.

He went on, "When you push a part of yourself away, when you push away any emotion you're feeling, it's bound to keep popping up. Like that beach ball, its counter-resistance will grow stronger in proportion to your efforts to shove it under the surface and out of sight. The energy it takes to sit on those uncomfortable feelings eventually drains your creativity and happiness, as well as the energy you could be using to contribute, as you say."

Ted gestured toward the water again. "See there, she stopped trying to control it."

Sophia noticed the little girl bobbing up and down near the colorful ball. She was no longer trying to push it underwater.

"When you shift your relationship with *your* beach ball—your troubling thoughts and emotions—and just allow them to float alongside you like she's doing, they'll just float there for a while and eventually drift away. A wind might come up, sure, and that ball might move in an unexpected direction, but if you don't try to push it anywhere, it will float along next to you in a relatively peaceful way. Then you can move around freely, choosing to play with it or simply allowing it to float along nearby.

"So, my advice is to make friends with your beach ball!" Ted chuckled, then paused. "Make friends with yourself."

Sophia took a few more steps before turning toward him. She was vacillating between teasing Ted about his beach ball metaphor and allowing his point to sink deeper into her psyche. "Ted, are you saying my *discomfort* is part of my strong desire to be of service and help create a better world? That it's something I should appreciate and not avoid?"

"Yes, that's part of it. Whatever you care about is going to keep urging you on from within. At times it *can* get uncomfortable. But ultimately that's what gives you energy for action!"

Ted walked with his hands in his pockets. He pushed the toe of his sneaker under the edge of a broken shell, flipping it into the air.

"Sophia, I'm curious. Is there another part of you that you're pushing down?"

Sophia thought for a moment, frowning a little. "I don't like the feeling I have when I think about all the problems in the world. Everywhere you look, things are getting more complex and troublesome. I get frustrated, angry, judgmental—everything I *don't* want to be. Then I start trying to control things, I guess. I end up pushing down my emotions, forcing myself to not feel or worry."

Ted looked up. "Sophia, please don't retreat from your anger, or sadness, or any of your other feelings. It's all right to have them, you know. The key is to have your emotions while not letting them have you in the grip of the DDT."

He continued, "Your emotions are pointing to something you care about, guiding you toward something you want to change. Those difficult feelings can become fuel for making a powerful choice."

Sophia paused, pensive and solemn. She turned to Ted.

"We have so much work to do to help ourselves and the planet," said Sophia. "I worry that we humans won't change our ways.

"It's like we're living on borrowed time. I feel this keen urgency. Somehow, we've got to accelerate our ability to listen to one another with compassion and kindness and create systems that include everyone. You know, really solve our problems, not just keep putting Band-Aids on them."

"Sophia, that yearning is deep and true."

She continued, "I want to be a part of bringing about *real* change, Ted. Not the same ol', same ol' where we tinker around the edges of an issue. How do we make sure all people are included in the conversations affecting their lives?" Sophia asked. "How do we create a world that works for everybody?"

Ted's smile had a tinge of sadness in it. "You're asking important questions, my dear. I can see your heart is troubled, and yet it's your concerns, your complaints themselves, that will propel you forward. They're pointing you toward what you care about, and ultimately, toward the action it makes sense for you to take."

Ted stopped walking and looked up at the clear sky. Vast and blue, without a cloud. "The power and intelligence of the universe exists right here." Ted gently touched his heart.

"Our Creator essence is always ready, just waiting to guide us.

"We can access great wisdom if we listen to this Creator within. We know this deep down, and yet we constantly look for truth and fulfillment outside ourselves. We try to siphon happiness and fulfillment from others. We may feel a temporary elation from unchecked material gain. We may get puffed up for a while when we associate with people we believe are smarter, wiser, or more powerful than ourselves, hoping they will rescue us from uncertainty. But of course, that doesn't work."

Sophia nodded in agreement. "Thank you, Ted, for reminding me that wisdom is always available to us."

After a moment she asked, "How do you experience the Creator essence? I feel it's there, but I never seem to have the words to describe it."

"Well," said Ted, "I try to live in acknowledgment and acceptance of our Creator essence. Not just knowing it exists in myself, but remembering it's in everyone, even when it's not readily apparent."

As he said the words, Sophia felt them. "I've heard you talk about this before, Ted, but . . . what exactly IS that Creator essence? I'm not trying to poke holes here; I just really want to understand."

Ted gave a gentle nod. "The Creator essence is the formless, infinite intelligence that gives energy to all that lives. It's not a function of our individual ego or personality. We cannot destroy, or increase, or decrease the Creator essence in us—it simply is."

They continued walking in silence for a while. Clusters of beach grasses punctuated the small sand dunes, and although it was late in the season, a few flowers were still flourishing. Ted made his way over to a colorful patch.

"Beautiful. Purple coneflowers . . . echinacea." He smiled at Sophia.

"I love coneflowers," Sophia said. "I have some in my backyard at home."

"Our Creator essence is the intelligence within this flower," said Ted. "That impulse to grow is so deep in its DNA that, whenever there is fertile soil, water, and sunlight, the root of this plant will emerge in spring into a magnificent purple coneflower. It cannot do otherwise. It 'knows' its nature and lives to express itself in just this way."

Ted continued, "We humans have the same built-in intelligence. The innate power to progress, to grow and thrive—that's our Creator essence. Even when it seems to be dulled a bit, or dampened by the weather of life experience—even when we try to ignore it—that impulse to grow cannot be denied as our true nature."

Sophia repeated Ted's words, making them her own: "The Creator essence is the formless, infinite intelligence that is the spirit of all life. It's not a function of our individual personalities. We can't destroy, or increase or decrease, the Creator essence—it simply is." As she spoke, she felt the life in the words themselves.

"Kind of a revolutionary idea isn't it, Sophia?" Ted smiled. "Many of our human systems are built on the opposite idea—that we're fundamentally flawed. Entire cultures and systems are based on that notion, a false belief that has caused a great deal of suffering."

Sophia's mind was ablaze. "Can you imagine how completely different our world would be if everyone recognized that the same Creator essence lives in you and me, and lives in every human being, whatever their culture, religion, or gender?"

"It would be a far kinder world, certainly. Our conversations would be about how to nourish that Creator essence in each other. We would focus on how to sustain our mutual growth and continuous learning. My dear, our highest aim in this life is to deeply understand our Creator essence—in other words, to make friends with ourselves—so that we can see and experience its power within. Once we do that, we're able to understand and respect others, even when we disagree with their views.

"I have realized a *few* things in my old age . . . ," Ted added with a smile. "One is this: Each new moment is a chance to appreciate and give thanks for the Creator essence—the wondrous wisdom that resides in all."

"Ted! Sophia! Over here!"

They looked up. Standing near the big boulder was Tara, joyfully waving her arms.

# 15

## Who Do You Want to Be?

Ted and Sophia walked quickly to greet a laughing Tara, who seemed to be concealing something behind her back. "I'm pleased it worked out for us to meet a bit later," she said. "Paco continues to rally and is having a good day. His spirits are high, and it was a blessing to spend a little more time with him today."

"Of course, Tara. I'm glad you chose to be with him," said Sophia.

Tara brought her right hand around from behind her back and revealed what she had been hiding. "Ted, here's your walking stick! You left it in my car the last time we walked here."

Ted threw his hands in the air, beaming. "Oh, there it is! Thank you, Tara. I thought I'd lost my old buddy forever!" Ted grinned as he took the stick. "I had completely forgotten where I left it," he said, lovingly inspecting its knots and grooves.

Tara explained to Sophia how, before setting out on their walk a few weeks earlier, she had parked her car near the big boulder, while Ted left his old truck near the trailhead. A sudden rainstorm had engulfed the beach that day, so, rather than get soaked, Ted had accepted a ride from Tara. In the hasty switch from her car to his truck, he had forgotten to grab his walking stick.

Ted held the stick high, examining it. The round knob at the top seemed made to fit the palm of his hand.

With an air of authority, he planted the walking stick in the soft ground. As if on cue, the three friends turned to head back down the stretch of sand that Ted and Sophia had just traveled. This part of the beach itself was like an old friend. The three had walked this route many times over the years, to and from the trail that began near Sophia's favorite cottage, out to the big boulder, and back again.

That stroll was ever-changing: the tide ebbing and receding, small birds hopping about in the surf. Further up on the sand were tall thickets of waving seagrass and long ropes of seaweed, clam shells, and jagged rocks spotted with barnacles, all of it shifting and evolving. Though the beach appeared different on each visit, a sameness remained. Whatever the weather, Sophia felt good there.

Tara smiled at Ted's excitement. "If I had known you would be so concerned about your walking stick, I'd have called you. My apologies."

The three continued walking, watching their feet as they pushed into the sand and onward. Then Tara looked up, pointing toward the advancing gray clouds. "Looks like we're in for some rain again."

After a pause Tara said, "I'm sure you two were having a fine conversation. Please continue!"

Sophia jumped in. "I was just hearing more about Ted and how he got so wise! It probably won't surprise you either that we were talking about the DDT roles. What I like about them is how they help me feel that everything that happens is natural and good, if I am willing to accept it—if I just stay curious about what I can learn from my reactive habits."

Ted nodded. "And if we understand it's natural for drama to come up from time to time, then we may stay in the DDT long enough to notice how the roles are unfolding in our minds and hearts. We begin to see how they distort our inner landscape. The only way to become familiar with our DDT patterns is to stick with them awhile and observe them. Sit with them," Ted said, adding, "It's not always easy.

"If we remain open to the fears that trigger our DDT, we learn not to reject our thoughts and feelings. But if we tell ourselves those drama roles are bad, if we hate them or try to pretend they're not operating, we miss out on learning what our patterns have to teach us."

Tara nodded her head. "We human beings can get in our own way— that much is clear. We seem to work so hard to protect ourselves from the very things we most need to learn."

"Like living in a castle with a moat and alligators!" Sophia chimed in, quickly adding, "I know that didn't make any sense, Ted. But I can explain. Tara knows how one of my clients compares her habit of self-protection to building a castle around herself, guarded by a moat full of alligators! I've felt that way myself at times, actually."

"Oh dear." Ted grimaced. "My sympathies.

"I'm grateful that our DDT habits are so insistent on making themselves known," he added. "With a little luck and persistence, though, eventually we no longer fall Victim to them."

"Oh my! There's a perspective!" said Sophia. "To be *grateful* for the DDT. I can see the wisdom in that!"

Tara smiled. "What would this world be like if we trusted our feelings instead of trying so hard *not* to feel? As I've walked with Paco in his illness, it's clear there are no 'bad' emotions to be suppressed, only unskillful reactions to them. Sadness, anger, and fear have so much to teach us."

"Quite true, Tara," Ted agreed. "I've learned that our emotions are like guides, showing us something we care about, or something we may be missing. They urge us to take meaningful action."

Sophia turned to Tara. "Do you remember how, on our last call, I shared my concern about the state of humanity—about our relationship to one another and to the Earth? Ted and I were just revisiting that."

Sophia shook her head. "It's almost like, if we step outside these self-punishing 'norms' and into self-compassion, or even just simple self-care, society encourages us to shame ourselves—and others too. There's this idea that the 'winners' in the world are perfectly in control, without any internal conflict. If you appear otherwise, you're viewed as lacking confidence—or worse, as incompetent, a loser." She rolled her eyes.

Ted added, "Yes, such challenges do exist. There are also moments of awe and joy. But when things go well, we rarely pause to appreciate the fact. We barely take notice of the good. We have a habit of constantly pushing ahead, caught in a drive to *have* more and *do* more, never feeling satisfied. That habit doesn't leave much room to rest and enjoy life."

"That's exactly how I feel right now!" exclaimed Sophia. "I have so many good things in my life, but I feel a constant pressure to make it even better."

"Hmm." Ted smiled. "Where does that pressure seem to be coming from?"

Sophia smiled and chuckled. "Well, I guess it's coming from *me*! I've been thinking of that pressure as coming from outside forces like society, but in the end, I suppose *I'm* the one putting pressure on myself."

Sophia reached into her coat pocket and pulled out a small disposable water bottle. She held up the battered piece of plastic.

"I found this on the trail. I know these are terrible for the environment, but at home I drink sparkling water from a bottle just like this one every day. And I end up feeling like I'm a dreadful person because I keep buying this stuff in plastic bottles." She searched her friends' faces.

"Well, of course you're not a dreadful person," said Ted, "although there may be habits you want to change. You mentioned feeling there's little you can do to impact the big problems we face. It's pretty common to fall Victim to the way we persecute ourselves sometimes."

"Well," said Sophia, "hearing you say that, I remember those powerful questions: 'What am I focusing on?' and 'What do I want?'"

Ted nodded. The three continued walking, and Sophia contemplated the questions. With each step, her clarity seemed to grow until at last she blurted out, "I want to embrace the beauty and wonder of this human experience . . . with all its foibles and flaws."

Tara had been silent for some time. Now she spoke firmly: "Sophia, we've been friends for a long time. My heart soars as I hear you speak today about loving your human experience even in difficult times.

"The tide is coming in," observed Tara. "In a few hours it will complete this cycle and then recede. Life is constantly moving, always flowing in to fill the space between what we see in front of us and what will soon become our future."

She slowed to a stop. Sophia and Ted stopped walking, too. A blue heron stood in the water, motionless. The bird's neck formed an S shape as it gazed ahead with singular focus.

Tara leaned in and whispered, "He must have his eye on supper." Sophia and Ted smiled in silent agreement.

Suddenly the heron took off, flying low over the water, head down, its eyes penetrating the waves. The three friends watched until the regal bird was out of sight, then turned and continued walking.

Ted was the first to speak. "So remarkable, these moments.

"Tara, I liked your observation . . . about the constant flow of life, about walking with whatever arises. How do we relate to the tension in that gap, between what we see now and our visions for the future? For me, this is when the DDT roles are most useful. If I begin to feel powerless or helpless in the face of that tension, I can be at risk of taking on the Victim role."

"At the same time," he went on, "if I push against that tension, I may get caught in the struggle of trying to control it, as we do in the Persecutor role. And if the Rescuer role emerges, I may become pleasing and helpful, hoping I can numb the tension, and it will just go away."

Ted paused, then added, "How we relate to that in-between space is so important. You described it beautifully, Tara. Nothing stands still or stays the same . . . and today the world appears to be changing faster than ever!"

"Yes, Sophia and I received some help with that yesterday," said Tara. "We were graced with the presence of two eagles feeding at low tide. We talked about what we can learn from the way Eagle flies into the wind, using that power to go the way he wants to go."

"Two eagles? How wonderful," said Ted.

"To leverage that energy in the gap, we first have to recognize its creative force. That may be the toughest part of being fully human—embracing what is uncomfortable, not knowing how things will turn out, yet continuing to move forward."

Ted looked down at the sand. He began playfully taking tiny steps, heel to toe, heel to toe, his hat bobbing along in rhythm with his feet. Tara and Sophia looked at him quizzically.

"Baby steps! That's the way!" Ted exclaimed, raising his arms joyously. "I know, I'm pretty silly sometimes," he said, grinning. "And of course, baby steps are *very serious business*.

"If we waited until we had all the answers, we'd never take action. Especially in a world as unpredictable as ours. Taking baby steps to get yourself into action helps you trust the creative process. You don't have to have it all figured out. You can just take one baby step, then another, and another, and then pretty soon you've walked all the way down the beach!" He laughed.

"Listen to you both!" said Sophia. "I'm so lucky to have such good friends." Her voice choked with emotion as her heart swelled with love and gratitude for all that Tara and Ted had shared with her. The feeling rippled through her body.

Energized, Sophia continued, "I want to accept the wonder and beauty that is all around me. That is my desired outcome and the focus for my life. But it's tricky business because, at the same time, I don't want to deny the things I need to pay attention to, like the ways I get triggered. Yet I still sometimes feel as if I'm drowning in my own drama!"

She paused and looked at the sky. A wall of gray clouds was moving toward the beach. Sophia wasn't ready to end her time with Tara and Ted, but the rain might soon force a goodbye.

"I'm watching them, too," said Tara, glancing up at the darkening sky.

"Shall we take a pivot and head back?" Ted asked.

"Sure," said Sophia absently, as all three friends turned, changing direction as if pulled by an invisible current.

"Sometimes I get paralyzed with worry or fear," she admitted, "and then I end up doing nothing. Do either of you ever have trouble deciding what baby steps to take? I mean, there are so many possibilities!"

"Great question," said Ted, "because you need to make decisions, don't you? When I have a hard time deciding, I usually pause to get clear about the *outcome* I want.

"And in regard to your question about how to choose a baby step," he added, "I offer you this: Keep your focus on what you truly care about. When you do that, the baby step you can take to move closer to your outcome will make itself known. Doing more of what is working is a principle I've followed that has helped me to decide which baby step to take."

Sophia wondered to herself if it could really be that easy.

She must have looked doubtful, because Ted added, "Truly! You can trust the magic of baby steps and let go of having to plan every detail in advance. Creating is a step-by-step process. As you keep moving forward, new and important information emerges. Sophia, you can trust the creative process."

The three walked awhile. The sun was nearing the horizon and the sky began to darken. Ted stumbled on a dip in the sand, and instinctively Sophia and Tara stopped short on either side of him and reached for his elbows.

"Thank you!" he said brightly. "I quite appreciate the support." Ted planted his walking stick deeper, rebalancing himself, then added with a twinkle, "I think the larger question here is, who do you want to be, on your way to what you want?"

Sophia thought about it. As she walked, she repeated to herself: "Who *do* I want to be, on the way to what I want?" Her heart was pounding with joy, considering that question. But she had come to expect that to happen when she hung out with Ted and Tara. She wondered what Tara was thinking.

"Sophia . . . ," Ted said softly, breaking her reverie, "Is there an example in your life that shows you who you want to be?"

She paused and wiggled the toe of her sneaker until it disappeared into the sand, then pulled it out again. She gazed out at the sky. "Yes, I think so. But I'd better tell you fast. I think that rainstorm will be right overhead in a few minutes." Tara and Ted looked up and nodded their agreement.

"Well," said Sophia, "one of my secret desires has been to learn to paint, but I kept hearing this critical inner voice saying, 'Why are you even doing this? You're not a good painter.'

"So, I kind of gave up. I put my paint and brushes away and set aside my goal to paint, or at least thought I did. But then last year I decided I really wanted to take another painting class. Then I realized my goal to paint a picture 'good enough to show to friends' was a *problem-focused* goal. It wasn't about what I wanted; it was about solving my imagined problem of *not being impressive enough*. A made-up problem that could never be solved. Just a self-judging thought, really. And I realized it wasn't serving me. So I stopped asking myself whether my paintings were impressive enough and shifted my focus. I started asking myself a new question: 'What kind of person do I want to be, while I'm learning to paint?'

"What a different feeling that was! The answer gradually emerged, and I made this declaration to myself: 'I am a person who enjoys being around others who like to paint. My pulse quickens when I walk into an artist's studio. I feel the childlike joy of playing with colors and shapes. I am a person who longs to paint.'"

Ted and Tara smiled and nodded. The friends continued walking in silence, glancing frequently at the clouds moving in.

Sophia went on, "When I shifted my focus to *being* someone who enjoys painting and longs to do it—that felt more interesting and more expansive. It wasn't about getting something, like finishing a painting I could show others for their approval. It was just about being myself, enjoying the creativity of painting. And it was a lot more fun."

"That's a beautiful example, Sophia!" said Ted. "When you focus on a broader purpose, it acts as a compass that guides you, even when things don't go the way you expect them to. And it's a more enjoyable approach than compulsive to-do lists that admonish us to do more, do better, and try harder."

Sophia took a deep, luxurious breath. She was understanding herself in a way that made her feel more confident. She knew she must have heard Ted, as well as Tara, say these things before. And yet suddenly it all felt new and somehow clearer.

"Talking about this has helped me a lot. I think what you both are pointing out is that we don't have to try to feel good all the time. And we don't always have to be striving after goals and accomplishments. The way I've been pressuring myself, it's like . . . even *thinking positively* was getting to be a stressful project!" She laughed.

"Pushing myself harder has never worked anyway. It only stopped me from learning to simply be with myself and my emotions. Meditation, journaling, slowing down, having more compassion for myself, and being with you two dear friends . . . all these gifts are teaching me how to connect with my Creator essence."

Sophia reached out her hand: raindrops. The clouds had arrived. She spotted the big boulder, their landmark, just ahead.

She turned and looked into the eyes of her friends. "Thank you, Ted. Thank you, Tara. I am grateful for you both. Your mentoring—your *friendship*—supports me more than I can say."

"You're welcome!" said Tara with a warm smile. She pulled her hood up over her head. "Well, it's time I headed back. Sophia, I look forward to our next call. Please drive safely as you return home tomorrow. Until then, have courage. Just as this wild man here says, your heart's wisdom will guide your steps."

They all laughed. Tara put her hands together at her heart and bowed to Sophia. "To the Creator in you."

Then, facing Ted, Tara raised her folded hands to her forehead. "To the Creator in you, my friend. I trust I'll see you again soon." With that, she turned and headed toward her car.

Sophia and Ted watched her walk a short way, then turned to each other, two big smiles mirroring their shared love for their friend.

"Well, let's get this old walking stick moving!" said Ted. "Maybe we can get you to your cottage and me back to my truck before the downpour starts." They picked up their pace and soon arrived at the fork in the trail, one path leading to Sophia's cottage and the other leading out to the parking lot.

Ted gently touched Sophia's shoulder. "My friend, only listen patiently, and you'll know what steps to take. You, and no one else, have the power to discover what's best for you." He gripped his walking stick and placed a hand over his heart. "To the Creator in you." He smiled. "I believe in you, my dear."

Sophia watched Ted as he lumbered up the trail. Tears welled up as she watched him go. She silently wished him a long life, and safe footing.

\* \* \*

"My last night at the cottage!" she thought wistfully as she hung up her damp jacket. She changed into drier clothes, thankful she hadn't gotten completely drenched. Sophia listened to the raindrops pelting the roof.

It had been warm all weekend, but tonight a chill had set in with the wet weather. In the basket next to the fireplace were bundles of kindling and dry wood, and Sophia gratefully used them to light a small fire. She made a cup of tea, wrapped a cozy blanket around her shoulders, and curled up on the couch.

Sophia loved nighttime at the cottage, the inky sky free of city lights. The wind and rain soon cleared, leaving a dark canvas speckled with stars.

As she watched, orange and blue flames rose up and danced in the fireplace, pouring heat into the little room. Sophia felt warmed on all sides, and she glowed with a warmth from within.

# 16

## Within Each Heart
## a Hidden Voice

Sophia stood in the doorway to her home office, gazing at the newest addition to the cluster of mementos atop her desk.

The day after returning from her beach retreat, Sophia had gone out to the local farmer's market. As she browsed a watercolor artist's booth, a greeting card had caught her eye. It featured a child in a red swimsuit, standing in the ocean surf, holding a rainbow-colored beach ball! Thrilled at her find, Sophia bought the card immediately. It now had taken its pride of place on her desk.

Appreciating the ocean scene on the card, Sophia relived Ted's telling of the beach ball story. Recalling that metaphor had since come to her aid in a few tricky situations where, before, she might have tried to stuff her emotions "underwater." She smiled. Remembering it all now seemed to bring Ted into the room: the sound of his warm voice and musical laugh as he raised his walking stick high in the air for effect.

Sophia had returned from the beach to a full practice of coaching clients. Now she was intentionally slowing down to take more time for the things that brought her joy. Her plan for next spring's larger-than-ever flowerpot garden was taking shape. She had ordered a full complement of bulbs to plant, and the thought of new colors and varieties of blooms excited her. On her laptop, Sophia had changed the screen saver to a brilliant display of tulips and added a quote: "'Earth laughs in flowers.' —Ralph Waldo Emerson."

One particular moment with Ted now came vividly to mind—when Sophia had pulled out that plastic water bottle and confessed that using something so environmentally unfriendly made her feel she was "a dreadful person." Ted hadn't taken the bait, only gently suggested that maybe there were habits she wished to change.

Sophia had, in fact, begun to change many of those habits. She had begun buying local products with less packaging and was passing up drinks sold in plastic bottles. She had even taken an online class about how to reduce her consumption, and now, one Saturday a month, she joined a group of volunteers to help pick up trash on local beaches and in public parks. Instead of merely complaining and worrying about the sorry state of the world, she was pleased to be taking responsibility for her own actions and doing her part where she could. These were small baby steps, but it felt good to be focusing on what she could contribute, rather than complaining.

Tara called one afternoon to share that Paco had died a week earlier. The family had cared for him at home until he passed, and Tara had remained by his side until his last breath. She reported that Paco's celebration of life had been filled with humorous stories about her brother, and about how he had made people feel loved and appreciated.

"I miss him so much," said Tara. "He was my best friend, my fishing buddy . . ." Her voice trailed off for a moment. "My brother stands with the ancestors now."

\* \* \*

In early spring, at Gabe's enthusiastic invitation and as a birthday gift to herself, Sophia had gone to Boulder to visit her son.

Sophia could see Gabe was happy. He was thriving at work and had a new girlfriend named Alana whom he had met playing co-ed softball. "I'm lucky you cleaned my closet, Mom. If you hadn't dug out my old ball glove and sent it to me, I might not have joined the softball team. And then," he added with a grin, "I would have missed out on meeting Alana."

Sophia could hear the excitement in his voice. "We've both practiced indoors all winter to get ready for spring league. She's a lot of fun to be with . . . plus, she's a great catcher!" He chuckled. She felt pleased as she listened. Clearly her son and this young woman had already developed a strong bond.

"I hope I can meet her, Gabe," said Sophia. "When the time is right, of course."

"Oh, you will, Mom. Definitely!" he said, beaming.

Gabe's apartment was sparse but well cared for and reasonably clean, Sophia thought. She had taken note of his hiking boots parked just inside the front door, and his ski pole rack mounted on the wall. A stunning photo poster of the snow-covered Rocky Mountains hung over a well-worn couch. Without a doubt, this was the home of an outdoorsman!

As soon as Sophia had set down her bag on the wobbly dining table, she noticed the birthday mug sitting on the kitchen counter.

Sophia smiled. "So, you like your mug, Gabe?"

"It's great, Mom. I have my morning coffee in it every day," he said.

Sophia turned the hefty sand-colored mug in her hands, inspecting the quote painted on one side: "Make Friends with Yourself." Gabe walked over and directly faced his mom.

"I see those words every day and they remind me of you." Gabe smiled. "That mug reminds me to treat myself like a friend, to be kind to myself. You've taught me a lot, Mom. I wouldn't be the person I am without you." Gabe put his hands on her shoulders and pulled her into a gentle hug.

"In fact, without you I wouldn't be here at all. So double thanks!

"And, speaking of birthday mugs, happy birthday to you! So great you came to visit me, on *your* birthday. Hey, check it out—I even wrapped this myself," said Gabe with a grin, handing her his present. Sophia took the colorful package and saw just how much Scotch tape it had taken to cover the uneven corners. Gabe had never been a gift wrapping kind of guy, and this touching attempt warmed her heart.

As she tore open the paper, Sophia stole a glance at her smiling son. She fumbled a little while opening the box, then gently slid out a picture frame. Her hand leaped to her mouth as she recognized the framed quote. Slowly, Sophia read it out loud:

"It remains the dream of every life to realize itself, to reach out and lift oneself up to greater heights. A life that continues to remain on the safe side of its own habits and repetitions, that never engages with the risk of its own possibility, remains an unlived life. There is within each heart a hidden voice that calls out for freedom and creativity."

That quote, by the Irish poet John O'Donohue, had long been one of Sophia's favorites. It described so well how the Creator wisdom could always be heard within, if she only listened. She held the frame to her chest. "Oh Gabe. This is beautiful. And this frame! It's the traditional Celtic knot," she said, tracing the repeating pattern with her fingers. "You're so thoughtful—you know I've always loved this quote." She set down the frame and gave her son a tender squeeze.

"When I get home, this is going right on my desk!"

"If you can find room for it," said Gabe with a chuckle. Sophia laughed, nodding. As her home office crowded with memorabilia revealed, she was a sentimental sort. And she liked that about herself.

\* \* \*

Sophia returned home from her visit with Gabe basking in the joy of seeing that her son had grown into a caring young man. Although still tired from her trip, she was eager to capture her thoughts and emotions—all that was swirling in her mind and heart in the wake of their visit. After changing clothes and unpacking a few things, she left the half-full suitcase for later. Easing into bed, she reached for her journal and started writing.

*I feel fulfilled and proud of how Gabe has grown up. He has entered a whole new stage of life now. And I sense that I too am entering a new phase of life. Self-doubts that plagued me for so long are no longer dominating my thinking. The craving, the drive to be more and do more, has calmed down. I still care, of course. In some ways, I care more than ever, but I no longer feel the weight of the world is on my shoulders. I will take responsibility for and find joy in doing my part to create a better and more just world. But I also know I cannot be of service to anyone unless I take care of myself. Instead of focusing on something "out there" that I think I need to fix, I have learned to "empty my vessel" so I can hear my inner wisdom. That's what Tara's mother taught her, and I am so grateful that she passed it on to me.*

*If I told my story about how I transformed my self-doubt—the need to please and fix the world—it wouldn't be a page-turner. There wasn't some special day when a miracle happened. I have made progress in fits and starts, by taking baby steps, with the support of my patient mentor, Tara, and my kind teacher, Ted. I care about making a meaningful contribution. I've learned, though, that if I am to offer anything that will last, first I have to unlock my joy.*

*I'm still no stranger to worry and fear. They will always be with me, I guess, and I may get triggered and slip into the DDT more often than I would like. But now I know a secret: I can accept all parts of myself and even see my drama habits as a gift, because those habits themselves are showing me the way.*

*If I didn't care about anything, I would never be stuck in the drama! So, when my drama buttons are pushed, I can pause, listen to those inner voices, and get really curious about what my life is trying to teach me. I can get curious about my unexpressed needs in order to find out what got me triggered in the first place. My desire is to see the light in every drama, to be open and willing to face it and release it.*

*My worthiness is right here, within me. It's not something I have to go looking to find, and it's not something I can earn by doing good deeds for others. That worthiness is always there. It is my Creator essence.*

*Like Gabe, I think I've actually learned to be friends with myself! About time, Sophia!* ☺

*Thank you, Ted. You showed me that, through personal reflection, listening to my inner wisdom, I can find my way. Since our visit, that beach ball card on my desk reminds me not to push away any part of me, not to resist the experience of my life in any given moment.*

*And thank you, Tara. I feel more prepared now to be the kind of coach I've always wanted to be. To boldly step into the roles of Creator, Challenger, and Coach, working with leaders who are ready to do their own work.*

Sophia put down her journal and turned out the light. It had been a wonderful birthday weekend.

\* \* \*

A few days later, on a beautiful spring afternoon, Sophia had wrapped up work early. As she sat on the front porch pulling on her walking shoes for a long jaunt around the neighborhood, the phone rang. The screen showed a local area code and number but no name. She rarely answered unidentified callers, but this time her intuition told her to answer.

"Hello?" she said, "This is Sophia."

"Sophia, this is RJ," said her former client, breathlessly. "Gosh, I'm so glad you picked up. I really need your help."

"It's good to hear from you," a surprised Sophia said politely.

RJ didn't hesitate. "It's serious, Sophia. I really need your help. Frankly, I'm at a complete loss."

"What's going on, RJ?"

"John *quit*! Remember John—our director of construction? He was the one I told you was always late for our Monday meeting."

Sophia remembered John well. During their coaching sessions, RJ had revealed how his lateness had triggered a harsh reaction. Sophia recalled with sadness how RJ had admitted resorting to embarrassing John in front of other team members in a desperate attempt to force him to be on time.

"Yes, I remember John, and the complaint you had about his being late. And I remember you did the Three Stories exercises around that. But I didn't personally meet him," said Sophia.

"Well," continued RJ, "John came in this afternoon for our weekly meeting. Things were going well—very well, in fact—from my perspective. Business is great and John's very popular with everyone. And since it was such a good meeting—nothing contentious or upsetting or awkward in any way—I took the opportunity to remind John again to be sure to be on time for our leadership meeting next Monday."

RJ's voice now rose with panic. "It was so *shocking*, Sophia! I still can't get over it. Do you know what John *did*?!" She didn't wait for an answer.

"He leaned forward and *slammed* my desk with both hands! It was so loud, I actually jumped. He was *really mad*. I'm telling you, I saw a side of John today I've never seen before.

"And then he yelled, 'That's it. I quit!' He just folded up his notebook, jumped up from his chair, and shouted, 'There's *no way* I'm going to take another week of this disrespect! I'll have my things out of my office by the end of tomorrow, and you'll have my resignation letter on your desk in the morning. *Goodbye*, RJ!'

"Sophia, I just can't get over it. He absolutely exploded. This quiet, mild-mannered guy, and he just *blew up*, you know? I was in shock. But somehow I got up from my desk and hurried after him. Before he got to the door, I said, 'John, *wait*. You can't *quit*. You're the director of construction. We're in the middle of a housing boom! *I need you!*'"

As she listened, Sophia flashed on the many other times her coaching clients had called her from the scene of a crisis. For years, those situations had triggered her to leap into the Rescuer role, thrilled at the chance to please her clients by solving their problems. Her Rescuer was very skilled at problem-solving and would quickly suggest the actions that her flustered, overwhelmed clients "should" take. Now Sophia felt that Rescuer role rearing its head again, that familiar urge to rush in and save the day. But she was determined not to let that pattern take over.

Sophia took a deep breath and acknowledged her desire to fix and please. She exhaled and let go of the impulse to suggest a solution.

"RJ is a Creator in her own right," she thought, "whether or not she knows it."

She began, "So then, RJ, what did John—" But before Sophia could finish, RJ interrupted.

"He said it was *too late*! That he was done with me and this job. I still can't believe it," she said.

There was a long pause. "I don't know what to do. I'm just in shock," RJ repeated.

Sophia could hear the fear in RJ's voice. Even over the phone, her breathing was audibly ragged and shallow. Sophia took another deep breath, calming herself a little more.

"RJ, thank you for reaching out. May I ask where you are calling from right now?"

"I'm in my office, sitting at my desk. Why?"

"I want to hear more in just a moment. First, though, let's take a few deep breaths and calm ourselves. You okay with doing that?"

"Sure," said RJ, in a barely audible whisper. It sounded as if she might cry.

"All right. Let's take three really deep belly breaths now. And let's hold those breaths a little longer than usual."

Together she and RJ practiced the deep breathing. As they did, Sophia's shoulders and neck relaxed, and she noticed she had tightened her jaw. She released the tension that had built up as she listened to RJ's anxious report.

Sophia soon felt a calmness wash over her body, the flow of energy returning. She relaxed her shoulders a bit more, resting at ease. She hoped RJ was feeling some relief as well.

"That felt good," affirmed RJ. "I feel a little better now. Thanks, Sophia." And with that, she launched into the grim details.

"So, after John left, I walked out of my office, and Maria, my assistant—remember Maria? Well, she was staring at me with a ghastly look on her face. And she silently mouthed the words 'What happened?' Obviously, she'd heard John yelling and saw him storming out of my office. I suspected she heard him yell that he had quit.

"Thank *heaven* no one else was around today! The leaders all left half an hour before, so it was just the two of us in the whole place, just me and Maria. So I pulled up a folding chair and sat down next to her desk. I hoped she might know something, you know? I asked her if she'd heard John yelling and she said yes, she had."

Any relaxation RJ had achieved with the deep breathing was rapidly disappearing.

She went on hurriedly, "So I said to her, 'Maria. Do you have any idea what made John act like that? He actually just *quit*, just like that!' And then Maria didn't answer for a long time . . . she kept looking away, like she didn't want to look me in the eye."

Suddenly RJ blurted out, "Do you think people are scared of me, Sophia?! Oh, never mind. Don't answer that," she added hastily.

Sophia listened as RJ went on, wondering where this story was going. She said to herself, "For now, just listen. Let her get it all out. Just be present, Sophia." She adjusted her posture a bit, to stay alert.

"Anyway," said RJ, "Maria finally told me what she knew. She said John has had a conflict on Monday mornings for months. His mother has Alzheimer's and is in a special care facility for people with severe memory loss. John and his wife love his mother dearly, and have promised to take care of her on the weekends, as long as she still recognizes them and is well enough to ride in the car to and from their home for visits. So anyway, every Friday evening, John's been picking his mother up at this facility and driving her to his house for the weekend. Then on Monday mornings he takes her back."

RJ paused. "Sophia, this is the really awful part. Maria told me John's late on Monday mornings because his mother has started refusing to go back to the facility after their weekend visits. And sometimes she won't get into his car. Maria said everyone at work knows about it and gives John a break. They know that when he's late, it's because his mother didn't want to go back to the memory care place and he got held up."

RJ sighed. "Sophia, I had no idea. I feel terrible. Everyone must have known this except me."

Sophia said gently, "RJ, why do you think you were the only one who didn't know why John was showing up late?"

"Well . . . I . . ." RJ stumbled searchingly. "I guess I never asked."

A long pause. "Wow," said RJ. "I never *asked* him why. Can you believe that? I just kept telling him not to be late for our Monday meetings.

"Ugh, I feel absolutely sick! It's like someone has carved out my heart or something. Like there's a hole in me, like something's really wrong with me. How could I *not even ask* him? How could I be so insensitive?

"And the last thing I said to him was, 'You *can't* quit. We're in a housing boom. I need you.' I wasn't thinking about what might be going on for him at all. I was only focused on myself and the company."

Nearly a minute passed in silence. For a moment Sophia thought the call might have dropped, but when she looked at her phone, she saw their connection was still good.

Sophia began, "RJ, that is quite a story. I'm sorry for your pain . . . and for John's difficult situation with his mother, too."

She paused for a long moment, then asked, "RJ, what is it that you want, right now?"

"I don't want to *feel* like this," said RJ shakily. "I feel so ashamed, like I'm an awful person and a terrible boss. I don't want to be so self-centered, only thinking about what's good for me, or what's good for the company, and never considering what other people might be going through."

"I hear you, RJ," said Sophia. "It takes courage to take responsibility for your actions. A lot of courage . . . and vulnerability."

RJ shot back, "I don't feel very *courageous*. But I do feel vulnerable, I guess.

"You know what's the worst part, Sophia? I had no one to call. I can't really talk to people here at work. I mean, it's pretty clear they don't trust me. And work has been my whole life for so many years I don't even have any friends."

She went on, her voice wavering. "I feel like my mom and sister just want me to bring home the profits. I feel . . . alone."

"It's good that you reached out," said Sophia. "It's completely understandable that you don't want to feel the way you're feeling right now."

"You asked me what I want," RJ said, her voice growing stronger. "Well, when we had our coaching sessions last year, there was this little voice inside me that kept saying, 'I know I can be a better person. I know I can be a better leader.' But I didn't want to hear that voice. I didn't want to see all the things about myself that I've kept hidden. So when you offered me the longer coaching program, I got scared, and I bolted.

"But I think I'm ready now," said RJ. "I mean, I've spent all of my adult life trying to honor my father and granddad, trying to run this business in a way that would make them proud. And they're not even *here*! I feel like a Victim of their expectations, and I don't want to feel that way anymore."

Sensing that RJ wanted to say more, Sophia held the silence. She stayed calm and said to herself, "Relax, Sophia. This is RJ's big choice point, not yours. There's nothing you need to do right now, other than be present with her, helping her create an accepting environment for her own reflection. No need to hurry or try to make this turn out a certain way. Just be still." She rolled back her shoulders, took a full breath, and continued to listen.

"I want *friends*," RJ insisted. "I want to have *fun*. I want a *life*!" she fairly shouted.

"That's a good start, RJ. And I sense there's more to that idea of what you want, possibly more than you realize. We all have an inner wisdom that's available if we're willing to listen and let it guide us."

"I don't think I can trust my inner wisdom, as you call it," said RJ. "At least not the way you trust *your* wisdom. I'd like to, though. I'd like to have what *you* have. I mean, you seem pretty steady."

"It's a journey, RJ," acknowledged Sophia. "And you are on that journey. We all are."

RJ's voice trembled as she asked, "Sophia, is the offer for that leadership coaching program still good? I think that's what I want."

Sophia smiled. She recalled the sting of rejection many months ago when RJ had said no to coaching. It had taken some time for Sophia to realize that secretly she had wanted to push RJ to change on *her* preferred schedule, rather than wait until RJ was ready.

"The Rescuer role isn't in charge here anymore," Sophia thought, smiling to herself. "No one changes on someone else's timetable. People change when they're ready to change."

"Yes, if you're ready, the offer is still good," Sophia said warmly.

"Well, I *am* ready," said RJ. "I'd like to start right now."

# Author's Note

It takes the humiliation of John slamming his hands on RJ's desk and announcing he's quitting for RJ to realize she needs some coaching to become the leader she wants to be. When she learns that she is the only one in her company who didn't know about John's ailing mother, RJ feels alone and full of shame. There is a gift in her pain, however. That pain acts as a Challenger to RJ, unlocking the grip of her family drama and giving her an opening to make the shift from leading with drama to leading with empowerment. Her coach, Sophia, recognizes that opening, and when Sophia asks the crucial question, "What do you want?" her client summons the courage to declare, "I want friends. I want to have fun! I want a life!"

Until that moment, RJ's focus has been confined to her drama story—about the kind of CEO she believes her father would have wanted her to be. Having held tightly to that narrative since the day she took charge of the family business, RJ has been locked in a prison of her own making. With Sophia's coaching, which shows her The Empowerment Dynamic, RJ gets a peek into the possibility of updating her human operating system, the possibility of a different way of living.

RJ's crisis with John turns out to be an opportunity for her to reach out. By asking Sophia for coaching support, she begins to let go of her protective armor. For RJ, as for all of us, the noble journey from Victim to Creator begins with facing what is missing in our lives, and then using that opportunity to clarify what we truly want. Only then can we move, with courage, toward our desired outcome.

What do *you* want? Is there a dream you have denied that you may not have acknowledged until now? If you accomplished that dream, how would you know it? As you lived that dream, how would you feel, what kinds of things would you say, and what would you want others to say about you?

Sophia dreams of making a meaningful contribution to the world yet feels overwhelmed by the world's endless troubles as she attempts to carry their full weight on her shoulders. Hoping to effect change, she decides she will coach influential leaders who can make the bigger contributions she cannot make alone. But Sophia becomes so strongly attached to being of service that soon even her wish to serve becomes a burden, hampering her aspiration to live a purposeful life. When things don't work out as Sophia plans, the clinging power of her attachment leaves her depleted, and she is thrown into a state of uncertainty and guilt.

Fortunately, Sophia has mentors. Tara and Ted help her to shift her focus away from struggling against the world around her and to move toward trusting her inner wisdom. As she connects with her natural joy and takes responsibility for self-care, Sophia makes the changes in her life that are hers to make—she makes an inner shift. In doing so, she learns that freedom comes from within, from her relationship with herself. She realizes that only when she knows and accepts herself fully will her desire to help be empowered to flow outward in effective support of others. By intentionally connecting with her Creator essence, Sophia begins to trust that inner wisdom to guide her steps.

Is there a Dreaded Drama story that has kept you locked in a kind of inertia? Like Sophia, are you intent on bringing a new story to life—one that is based on the wisdom inherent in your Creator essence? As you identify and embrace the drama story that blocks that essence, will you begin to let go of that drama story *now*, so that you're free to create a new and empowering story?

When we see a flashing red light on the dashboard of our lives, our first response is often fear and anxiety. We'd prefer to ignore that important, even urgent, information and the changes it might insist that we make. But part of our tender human journey is learning to welcome uncomfortable emotions and behaviors as helpers when they light up inside us. That means giving up the idea that our flashes of anger, sadness, or grief mean that we're somehow flawed or deficient. Because when we judge these natural aspects of our humanity as *wrong*, we're allowing ourselves only two choices. We can do as Sophia initially does and make ourselves into a project to be fixed, or we can act as if we're powerless to respond constructively to what life has thrown our way, as RJ initially believes. Both approaches land us in the Victim mentality, where we get stuck in drama, bouncing around in the DDT.

The Victim voice shouts, but the Creator voice whispers. When we trust our innate goodness and learn to give ourselves true self-care and compassion, The Empowerment Dynamic roles of Creator, Challenger, and Coach begin to emerge with clarity and strength. It often takes a traumatic event to help us realize how our reactive habits have kept us isolated in victimhood, unaware of the negative impact those habits have on us and on our loved ones and co-workers. But it is at these very moments, when the warning light is flashing, that we have the awesome power to transform our lives for the better. We only need to pause, give ourselves a break, and awaken our inner observer. Then we can coach ourselves with kindness. And we can begin to see the gift of wisdom hidden inside our drama.

# Acknowledgments

I am incredibly grateful for Ceci Miller (www.Cecibooks.com), who is a special friend and a gifted editor. Ceci recognized Sophia's voice hidden deep in my heart and inspired me to trust my inner wisdom as her story emerged. I appreciate Ceci's team, too: Thanks to Shannon McCafferty for your brilliant book design, to Kristin Carlsen for careful copyediting, and to Bob Lanphear for skillfully putting it all together in our final product.

Debbie Hulbert has done whatever is needed for over fifteen years to keep our company growing, from website design and maintenance to shipping books, to customer support, and so much more. Alicia Burson keeps everything running smoothly and efficiently, staying on top of each administrative detail. Thank you, Debbie and Alicia!

A special thank you to our community of certified 3 Vital Questions (3VQ) trainers, many of whom first joined us in this work over ten years ago. My heartfelt thanks to each of you for your enthusiasm for 3VQ and TED* (*The Empowerment Dynamic) as we learn and grow together. Thanks also to all my clients, with whom I honed my coaching skills and learned to fully appreciate myself as a coach.

Thank you to every coach and participant who took the early TED* for Coaches courses, launched a decade ago. Your enthusiasm for this work inspired me to keep teaching and to delve deeper into the unique coaching process made possible with The Empowerment Dynamic.

I am so grateful for the many fellow masterful coaches who are also dear friends and first readers. Your insights made this book far better. Special gratitude to Barb McAllister, my first co-facilitator in the original coaching course, and to Dr. Petra Platzer, Director of Georgetown University's Health and Wellness Coaching program, whose unique insights into the stages of psychological development guided me as I shaped Sophia and her family of characters. Thanks to Beth Davis and Jennifer Herold, whose unique perspectives helped me to shape the coaching dialogue and tools. A special thanks to Stephanie Davenport, who shared her invaluable insights about the Northwest Indigenous culture and helped shape the character Tara as a wise mentor and coach for Sophia. I am indebted to my longtime friend and colleague Dr. Ann Deaton for steadfast support as a first reader, fellow 3VQ trainer, and co-facilitator of our newest coaching courses.

Great gratitude to Master Coach Molly Gordon, my first coach and one of the original first readers for David's book, *The Power of TED*. Your encouragement has helped me keep listening to my inner wisdom. Thanks to Dot Maver, who listened for my authentic voice and challenged me to show up with an open, trusting heart. Deep appreciation to Jerilyn

Brusseau, a special friend and confidant, for always listening and wanting me to succeed.

Amy Felix-Reese, your brilliance in co-facilitation is unmatched. I am humbled by your Foreword and endorsement of this work.

I am blessed to have such wonderful friends and support from my Wabi-Sabi sisters Bea Dixon, Susan Sweetwater, Cezanne Allen, Marcy Jackson, Mary Anne Keane, Julie Gardner, Jennifer Waldron, and Nancy McCaughey. Our conversations mean the world to me.

The gift of being "mamma" to my three adult children warms my heart beyond words. McKenzie, your consciousness and dedication to your profound spirit has been a guiding light on my own spiritual path. Your clever husband and gifted writer, Bill; your daughter, Charley; and soon-to-arrive grandbaby are so dear to me. Morgan, my kind and adventurous daughter, you show me what is most valuable in life every day. I've learned more from you than you can possibly know. And dear Carson, on your unique journey, becoming the young man you wish to be. I love our conversations and how we have grown up together.

Heartfelt gratitude to David Emerald Womeldorff, who first shared your epiphanies and insights with me and invited me to join you on this amazing journey together of life and work—to bring *TED*\* and *3 Vital Questions* to the world. I am so grateful for your presence, your gifts, and all that you have shared with me. As you so often say, "Here's to the Creator in you!"

# Suggested Reading

Almaas, A. H. *Diamond Heart Book One: Elements of the Real in Man*. Boulder, CO: Shambhala, 1987.

Beck, Martha. *The Way of Integrity: Finding the Path to Your True Self*. New York: The Open Field, 2021.

Berger, Jennifer Garvey. *Unlocking Leadership Mindtraps: How to Thrive in Complexity*. Stanford Briefs, Stanford University Press, 2019.

Boyatzis, Richard, Melvin Smith, and Ellen Van Oosten. *Helping People Change: Coaching with Compassion for Lifelong Learning and Growth*. Boston: Harvard Business Review Press, 2019.

Chodron, Pema. *Living Beautifully with Uncertainty and Change*. Boulder, CO: Shambhala, 2012.

Emerald, David. *3 Vital Questions: Transforming Workplace Drama*. Bainbridge Island, WA: Polaris, 2019.

Emerald, David. *The Power of TED\* (\*The Empowerment Dynamic)*. 10th Anniversary ed. Bainbridge Island, WA: Polaris, 2016.

Franklin, Marion. *The HeART of Laser-Focused Coaching: A Revolutionary Approach to Masterful Coaching*. Wilmington, DE: Thomas Noble Books, 2019.

Hawkins, David R. *Letting Go: The Pathway of Surrender*. Carlsbad, CA: Hay House, 2012.

Hendricks, Gay. *The Big Leap: Conquer Your Hidden Fear and Take Life to the Next Level*. HarperOne, 2009.

Kegan, Robert, and Lisa Laskow Lahey. *Immunity to Change: How to Overcome It and Unlock the Potential in Yourself and Your Organization*. Boston: Harvard Business School Press, 2009.

Manning, Ken, Robin Charbit, and Sandra Krot. *Invisible Power: Insight Principles at Work*. Lexington, MA: Insight Principles, 2015.

McLean, Pamela. *Self as Coach, Self as Leader: Developing the Best in You to Develop the Best in Others*. New York: Wiley, 2019.

Moffitt, Phillip. *Dancing with Life: Buddhist Insights for Finding Meaning and Joy in the Face of Suffering*. New York: Rodale, 2008.

Mohr, Tara. *Playing Big: Practical Wisdom for Women Who Want to Speak Up, Create, and Lead*. New York: Avery, 2015.

O'Donohue, John. *To Bless the Space Between Us: A Book of Blessings*. New York: Doubleday, 2008.

Reynolds, Marcia. *Coach the Person, Not the Problem: A Guide to Using Reflective Inquiry*. Oakland, CA: Berrett-Koehler, 2020.

Singer, Michael A. *The Untethered Soul: The Journey Beyond Yourself*. Oakland, CA: New Harbinger, 2007.

Stanier, Michael Bungay. *The Coaching Habit: Say Less, Ask More & Change the Way You Lead*. Toronto, ON: Box of Crayons, 2016.

Stone, Hal, and Sidra L. Stone. *Embracing Our Selves: The Voice Dialogue Manual*. Novato, CA: New World Library, 1989.

# Books in This Series

## Who Do You Want to Be
## On the Way to What You Want?
Coaching with The Empowerment Dynamic
by Donna Zajonc, MCC

**3 Vital Questions**
*Transforming
Workplace Drama*

by David Emerald

**The Power of TED\***
*(\*The Empowerment
Dynamic)*
by David Emerald

# Learn More about
# The Empowerment Dynamic

Check out our coaching courses, trainer
certification, bulk book purchase options,
eCourses, and more at
Center for The Empowerment Dynamic.

. . . . .

**www.TheEmpowermentDynamic.com**

. . . . .

Sign up for our Free Friday Blog at our website.
Email for more information at
**info@TheEmpowermentDynamic.com**

**D**onna Zajonc, MCC, is Director of Coaching for the Center for The Empowerment Dynamic. She is passionate about teaching and facilitating coaching courses based upon TED* (The Empowerment Dynamic). A Master Certified Coach, Donna received the Washington State excellence in coaching award in 2017.

Donna's love of community and leadership led her to public service early in her career. During that time, she served three terms in the Oregon legislature and was her party's nominee for Secretary of State. After leaving politics, she was owner and CEO of a multi-store food retail company in Portland, Oregon. Deeply curious about the inner landscape of the human mind, Donna fully embraced professional coaching in 2001, later joining her husband, David, in their **3 Vital Questions** and **The Empowerment Dynamic** leadership training and facilitation. She lives in the Pacific Northwest region of the US, where she enjoys daily beach walks, good books, sampling dark chocolate and robust microbrews, and hanging out with her children and grandchildren.